AI Digest

More of everything you wanted to know about AI but don't have time to read

VOLUME 2

Dr Darryl J Carlton

Technics Publications

SEDONA, ARIZONA

115 Linda Vista
Sedona, AZ 86336 USA
https://www.TechnicsPub.com

Edited by Sadie Hoberman

Cover design by Lorena Molinari

First Printing 2024

Copyright © 2024 by Dr Darryl J Carlton

ISBN, print ed.	9781634625289
ISBN, Kindle ed.	9781634625302
ISBN, PDF ed.	9781634625319

Contents

From the Author

Welcome back to the latest edition of AI Digest, your concise guide to cutting-edge developments in artificial intelligence. In a world where information overflows and time is scarce, this digest serves as your essential "reader's digest" for AI, distilling the insights of leading researchers and policy think tanks from across the globe.

Recent studies show that the median number of books read by adults annually is just four, with many readers still needing to complete those. Staying informed about rapidly evolving technologies like AI can seem daunting in our fast-paced society. That's where AI Digest comes in. My purpose in creating this digest is to provide you with easily consumable summaries that capture the essence of complex ideas and groundbreaking research.

For this edition, I've meticulously analyzed and condensed over forty documents from "What Think Tanks are Thinking," a directory published by the European Parliament. These summaries offer you a panoramic view of the AI landscape, touching on key developments, ethical considerations, and potential future impacts.

Each summary is crafted to give you the core concepts and critical takeaways, allowing you to grasp the big picture without getting lost in technical jargon. Whether you're a busy professional, a curious student, or simply someone interested in understanding how AI is shaping our world, these digests are designed to keep you informed and engaged.

I encourage you to use these summaries as a springboard for further exploration. Feel free to delve deeper when a particular report or topic piques your interest. Seek out the original documents, explore the suggested 'further readings,' and engage with the broader discourse surrounding these ideas.

In the meantime, let this carefully curated digest serve as your window into the thoughts and findings of some of the world's preeminent AI experts. AI Digest aims to keep you abreast of the latest developments in this transformative field from breakthrough algorithms to policy implications, from ethical debates to industry applications.

So, prepare to embark on an intellectual journey through the forefront of AI research and policy. Let's explore together how artificial intelligence is reshaping our present and molding our future.

Thank you for picking up my book.

I certainly hope you enjoy it!

Darryl Carlton
darryl.carlton@me.com
https://www.darrylcarlton.com

One

What Is Artificial Intelligence (AI)?

Noah Berman, Council on Foreign Affairs, December 2023

This report explores the fundamental aspects of artificial intelligence (AI), its development, and its far-reaching implications for the global economy, job market, climate change, national security, and governance. AI's rapid advancement poses both unprecedented opportunities and significant challenges, including ethical considerations and the potential for geopolitical shifts. This analysis draws from extensive research and expert opinions to comprehensively understand AI's current and future impact.

Key Findings

- **Definition and Evolution of AI:** AI refers to the ability of machines to perform tasks that typically require human intelligence. Its development has progressed from early theoretical work to sophisticated generative AI models like ChatGPT.

- **Economic Impact:** AI is projected to significantly boost global GDP, potentially adding $7 trillion annually by enhancing productivity and innovation.

- **Job Market Transformation:** AI could displace and create jobs, substantially impacting white-collar and lower-skilled positions.

- **Environmental Concerns:** AI's energy consumption and carbon footprint are growing concerns, though it also has the potential to mitigate climate change through efficiency improvements.

- **National Security:** AI's role in military applications and geopolitical competition, particularly between the US and China, is critical.

- **Governance Challenges:** Effective AI governance requires balancing innovation with ethical considerations and international cooperation.

Analysis

Definition and Evolution of AI

AI's roots trace back to the 1950s, when John McCarthy defined it as "the science and engineering of making intelligent machines." Since then, AI has evolved from basic computing functions to advanced generative models like ChatGPT, which can produce human-like text and content based on extensive training data.

Economic Impact

AI's integration into various sectors promises substantial economic benefits. Companies increasingly use AI for tasks such as automated customer service, targeted advertising, and algorithmic trading. The global GDP is expected to rise by an additional $7 trillion annually due to AI-driven productivity gains. Nations that embrace AI will likely gain competitive advantages, while those that resist may fall behind.

Job Market Transformation

AI's impact on the job market is multifaceted. While it may automate many tasks, leading to job displacement, it also creates new opportunities. For example, AI can enhance the productivity of less-experienced workers and support the development of new industries. However, the risk of job losses, particularly in white-collar sectors like accounting and marketing, remains significant.

Environmental Concerns

The environmental impact of AI, particularly its energy consumption, is a growing concern. AI models require substantial computational power, leading to high energy use and carbon emissions. However, AI also has the potential to improve energy efficiency and support renewable energy research, helping to mitigate its own environmental footprint.

National Security

AI is a key factor in the strategic competition between the US and China. Both nations are investing heavily in AI to gain economic and military advantages. AI's capabilities in autonomous weapons, strategic analysis, and cyber operations could transform the nature of warfare and national security. The potential for AI-driven disinformation campaigns also poses a significant threat to democratic processes.

Governance Challenges

Effective AI governance is crucial to balancing innovation with ethical considerations. International cooperation is essential to develop shared standards and regulations. The US, EU, and China have taken different approaches to AI governance, reflecting their unique priorities and values. Collaborative efforts, such as the G7's Hiroshima Process and the UN's AI Advisory Board, are steps toward establishing global AI governance frameworks.

Recommendations

- **Develop Comprehensive AI Governance Frameworks:** Establish international standards for AI ethics, transparency, and accountability.

- **Promote Sustainable AI Practices:** Encourage the use of renewable energy in data centers and invest in energy-efficient AI technologies.

- **Support Workforce Transition:** Implement policies to reskill workers affected by AI-driven job displacement and promote new job creation.

- **Enhance Public Awareness:** Educate the public about AI's benefits and risks to foster informed discussions and decision-making.

- **Foster International Collaboration:** Strengthen global partnerships to address the cross-border challenges of AI governance and ensure equitable benefits.

Conclusion

AI's rapid advancement presents both immense opportunities and significant challenges. Its potential to transform economies, job markets, and national security is matched by the ethical and environmental concerns it raises. Policymakers can harness AI's benefits while mitigating its risks by adopting proactive governance measures, promoting sustainability, and fostering international cooperation.

Further Reading

Noah Berman, "What Is Artificial Intelligence (AI)?" Council on Foreign Relations, 2024.

Daniel Castro, "Policymakers Should Use the SETI Model to Prepare for AI Doomsday Scenarios," Center for Data Innovation, 2023.

RAND Corporation, "The Promise and Peril of AI in the Power Grid," 2024.

Pew Research Center, "Slightly fewer Americans are reading print books, new survey finds," 2023.

Wilson Center, "AI Poses Risks to Both Authoritarian and Democratic Politics," 2024.

Two

Charting the geopolitics and European governance of Artificial Intelligence

Racula Csernatoni, Carnegie Europe, March 2024

This report examines the complex landscape of artificial intelligence (AI) governance in the European Union (EU) and its global implications. The EU faces significant challenges in balancing innovation with regulation while aiming to establish itself as an AI development and governance leader. Key issues include implementing the AI Act, the EU's technological sovereignty ambitions, and the impact of prevailing AI narratives on policy and public perception.

Artificial intelligence has rapidly evolved from a futuristic concept to a present-day reality, profoundly influencing global power dynamics, security considerations, and economic paradigms. This report analyzes the EU's multifaceted approach to AI governance, examining its efforts to navigate geopolitical, economic, and regulatory concerns while striving for global leadership in responsible AI development.

Key Findings

- **EU's AI Governance Approach:** The EU is implementing a risk-based regulatory framework through the AI Act. There's a focus on fostering "trustworthy AI" aligned with European values. The EU aims to establish a global standard for AI regulation.

- **Technological Sovereignty and Innovation:** A significant gap exists between the EU's ambitions and its current investment levels. The EU lags behind the US and China in AI funding and innovation. Initiatives like AI Watch and various EU funding programs aim to boost AI development.

- **Geopolitical Dynamics:** AI is increasingly viewed as a critical component of national security and economic power. The EU faces challenges competing with the US and China in the global AI race. There's a need for strategic partnerships and a unified EU foreign policy on AI.

- **Narratives and Public Perception:** Prevailing narratives of AI power and disruption significantly influence policy and public opinion. These narratives often serve powerful actors and may distract from pressing risks. There's a need for critical evaluation of AI narratives to establish realistic governance expectations.

- **Global AI Governance Landscape:** A complex web of regulatory frameworks is emerging worldwide. The EU must navigate this landscape while trying to establish its AI Act as a global benchmark. Challenges exist in aligning the AI Act with other international governance initiatives.

Analysis

The EU's approach to AI governance reflects its commitment to balancing innovation with ethical considerations and fundamental rights protection. The AI Act represents a pioneering effort to create a comprehensive regulatory framework for AI systems. However, the EU faces significant challenges translating its regulatory ambitions into global leadership.

The gap between the EU's technological sovereignty rhetoric and its actual investment in AI innovation is concerning. While initiatives like the European AI Alliance and various funding programs demonstrate commitment, more is needed to compete with the massive investments made by the US and China.

The geopolitical dimensions of AI development add complexity to the EU's efforts. As AI becomes increasingly central to national security and economic competitiveness, the EU must balance cooperation and strategic autonomy.

The power of AI narratives in shaping policy and public perception cannot be underestimated. While some narratives may drive innovation and investment, others may lead to misallocation of resources or distract from more immediate challenges. The EU must critically examine these narratives to ensure its governance approach addresses real rather than perceived risks.

The global AI governance landscape is rapidly evolving, with multiple initiatives and frameworks emerging. The EU's ability to influence this landscape will depend on its success in implementing the AI Act and forging strategic partnerships with like-minded nations.

Recommendations

- **Increase AI Investment:** The EU should significantly boost its funding for AI research and development to close the gap with global competitors.

- **Strengthen Unified Approach:** Develop a cohesive EU foreign policy on AI to present a united front in global governance discussions.

- **Enhance Stakeholder Engagement:** Improve inclusion of civil society and translate AI governance initiatives into accessible language for broader public engagement.

- **Future-proof the AI Act:** Ensure the AI Act's implementation is flexible enough to adapt to rapid technological advancements.

- **Foster Strategic Partnerships:** Cultivate alliances with key global partners to promote the EU's vision of responsible AI development.

- **Address Narrative Influence:** Develop strategies to critically evaluate and shape AI narratives to ensure they align with realistic governance goals.

- **Harmonize Global Efforts:** Work towards aligning the AI Act with other international governance initiatives to promote global coherence in AI regulation.

Conclusion

The EU stands at a critical juncture in AI governance. While its regulatory efforts, particularly the AI Act, position it as a potential global leader in responsible AI development, significant challenges remain. Bridging the investment gap, unifying its approach, and effectively navigating the complex global governance landscape will be crucial for the EU to realize its ambitions in the AI domain.

Further Reading

European Commission. "Artificial Intelligence Act." 2021.

Bradford, Anu. "The Brussels Effect: How the European Union Rules the World." Oxford University Press, 2020.

Maslej, Nestor et al. "Artificial Intelligence Index Report 2023." Stanford University, April 2023.

European Commission. "White Paper on Artificial Intelligence: A European Approach to Excellence and Trust." February 19, 2020.

Smuha, Nathalie A. "From a 'Race to AI' to a 'Race to AI Regulation'–Regulatory Competition for Artificial Intelligence." Law, Innovation and Technology, 2021.

THREE

The EU's AI Act Creates Regulatory Complexity for Open-Source AI

Daniel Castro, Center for Data Innovation, March 2024

The EU's Artificial Intelligence Act (AI Act) creates a comprehensive regulatory framework for AI systems, including some specific provisions for open-source AI. While the act attempts to exempt certain open-source AI projects from some requirements, many open-source AI initiatives will still face regulatory complexity under the new rules. This could hinder innovation and complicate the development of open-source AI in the EU.

Key Findings

- **Scope and Categories:** The AI Act categorizes AI systems into four risk levels: unacceptable, high, limited, and minimal risk. It bans unacceptable risk AI systems and imposes varying requirements on the other categories.

- **Open-Source AI Provisions:** Some exemptions exist for open-source AI, but they are limited in scope. Open-source AI is not exempt from bans on unacceptable-risk AI or restrictions on high-risk AI systems. Exemptions only apply if open-source products are not monetized.

- **General Purpose AI (GPAI) Models:** Open-source GPAI models face less stringent documentation requirements unless deemed to present systemic risk. All GPAI models must disclose training content information and comply with EU copyright law.

- **Regulatory Complexity:** Many open-source AI projects will still fall under the AI Act's rules. Compliance may be particularly challenging for decentralized open-source projects.

- **Scientific Research Exemption:** AI systems developed solely for scientific research are exempt from the rules. This creates a potential loophole for commercial repurposing of research models.

Analysis

The EU's attempt to balance innovation with regulation in the AI Act has resulted in a complex set of rules for open-source AI. While some exemptions exist, they are narrowly defined and may not cover many real-world open-source AI initiatives, especially those with any form of monetization. This could disadvantage European open-source AI projects compared to proprietary models or those developed outside the EU.

The act's treatment of GPAI models and the scientific research exemption also create potential inconsistencies and loopholes that may need to be addressed in future revisions or through regulatory guidance.

Recommendations

- **Clarify Exemptions:** Provide more detailed guidance on what constitutes "monetization" for open-source projects.

- **Review Impact:** Closely monitor the impact of the AI Act on open-source AI development in the EU.

- **Consider Amendments:** Be prepared to amend the Act if it proves overly burdensome for legitimate open-source AI projects.

- **Enhance Support:** Develop programs to support open-source AI initiatives in navigating the new regulatory landscape.

- **International Coordination:** Work with global partners to harmonize approaches to open-source AI regulation.

Conclusion

While the EU AI Act aims to create a safe and innovative AI ecosystem, its treatment of open-source AI creates significant regulatory complexity. Careful implementation and ongoing review will be crucial to ensure the Act does

not inadvertently stifle open-source AI innovation in
Europe.

FOUR

What to Expect from the Digital Markets Act

Zach Meyers, Centre for European Reform, March 2024

The Digital Markets Act (DMA) will transform the European digital landscape starting March 6, 2024. This report examines the DMA's implications for large tech firms, its potential impact on competition, and the challenges in its implementation. While the DMA aims to make digital markets more contestable and fair, its effects may be mixed, with some positive outcomes for competition balanced against potential unintended consequences and ongoing regulatory complexities.

The Digital Markets Act represents a significant shift in regulating large tech platforms in the European Union. This report analyzes the DMA's scope and initial implementation, and potential outcomes for digital competition and consumer choice in Europe.

Key Findings

- **Scope and Application:** The DMA regulates large tech firms' platforms, including operating systems, online marketplaces, messaging services, social media networks, browsers, and digital advertising services. Most major tech companies accept regulation of their flagship services, though some are appealing specific decisions.

- **Impact on Competition:** The Commission's approach to regulating services shows some nuance, potentially enhancing competition in certain areas. Some DMA rules may inadvertently strengthen already dominant players in certain markets.

- **Implementation Challenges:** Many aspects of DMA compliance are likely to be heavily disputed, potentially delaying benefits realization. Detailed economic questions about 'fair' practices may take years to resolve through litigation.

- **Ongoing Regulatory Scrutiny:** The DMA only addresses some competition concerns in the digital sector, particularly in digital advertising and cloud computing. Competition authorities are likely to continue investigations alongside DMA enforcement.

- **Global Implications:** The DMA may influence digital regulation globally, potentially benefiting tech firms if other countries adopt similar approaches.

Analysis

The DMA represents a bold attempt to reshape digital markets in Europe, but its impact is likely to be complex and multifaceted. While it introduces important new choices for consumers and opportunities for competitors, it also risks creating new regulatory challenges and may not fully address some existing competition concerns.

The Commission's nuanced approach to deciding which services to regulate shows promise, but the DMA's rigid structure sometimes leads to suboptimal outcomes. The law's implementation will likely be contentious, with disputes over compliance potentially delaying its full impact.

Recommendations

- **Monitor Implementation:** Closely track the DMA's effects on competition and consumer choice, adjusting approaches as needed.

- **Enhance Dispute Resolution:** Develop mechanisms for swiftly resolving compliance disputes to maximize the DMA's effectiveness.

- **Address Remaining Gaps:** Consider additional measures to tackle competition issues not fully addressed by the DMA, particularly in digital advertising and cloud computing.

- **Promote Global Coordination:** Engage with international partners to harmonize approaches to digital market regulation where possible.

- **Support Consumer Education:** Develop programs to help consumers understand and effectively use new choices provided under the DMA.

Conclusion

The Digital Markets Act marks a significant step in European tech regulation, potentially enhancing competition and consumer choice in digital markets. However, its success will depend on effective implementation, ongoing monitoring, and a willingness to address unforeseen consequences. As other countries consider similar regulations, the DMA's outcomes will likely influence global approaches to digital market governance.

Further Reading

European Commission. "The Digital Markets Act: Ensuring fair and open digital markets." 2023.

Crémer, J., de Montjoye, Y. A., & Schweitzer, H. "Competition policy for the digital era." European Commission, 2019.

Khan, L. M. "The separation of platforms and commerce." Columbia Law Review, 2019.

Caffarra, C., & Scott Morton, F. "The European Commission Digital Markets Act: A translation." VoxEU, 2021.

Cabral, L., et al. "The EU Digital Markets Act." Yale Tobin Center for Economic Policy, 2021.

FIVE

Quantum Computing: A blessing and a threat to our digital world

Ganesh Subramanya, Friends of Europe, March 2024

Quantum computing presents both transformative potential and significant cybersecurity risks for the EU. While offering breakthroughs in fields like drug development, it also threatens to undermine current encryption methods. This report examines the EU's readiness for quantum computing's impact on cybersecurity and recommends actions to prepare for a quantum-secure future.

Key Findings

- **Quantum Threat to Encryption:** Most current cryptographic keys are vulnerable to quantum decryption. EU's highly digitalized economy and services are particularly at risk.

- **EU Preparedness:** EU has ambitious quantum computing goals but lags in quantum cybersecurity readiness. Recent cybersecurity legislation (NIS II,

Cybersecurity Act, Cyber Resilience Act) does not explicitly address quantum threats.

- **International Context:** US has enacted the Quantum Cybersecurity Preparedness Act (2022). EU's EuroQCI[1] network protects critical government infrastructure but not wider citizen services.

- **Industry Challenges:** Many online service providers, especially SMEs, need more resources to assess quantum readiness. There is a need for streamlined regulations and explicit guidance on quantum cybersecurity policies.

- **Global Cooperation:** EU is well-positioned to lead international efforts in quantum-safe cryptography standards. A limited pool of quantum cybersecurity experts globally necessitates international collaboration.

Analysis

The EU faces a significant challenge in balancing its quantum computing ambitions with the need to secure its digital infrastructure against quantum threats. While some measures like EuroQCI are in place, there needs to be more protection for non-governmental services critical to citizens. The EU's strong position in cryptography and blockchain standards provides a foundation for leadership

---

[1] The European Quantum Communication Infrastructure (EuroQCI) Initiative is a secure communication infrastructure spanning the whole EU, including its overseas territories.

in quantum security, but requires more focused policy attention and resource allocation.

Recommendations

- **Expand Quantum Risk Assessments:** Support industries, especially SMEs, in evaluating their quantum readiness.

- **Enhance Regulatory Framework:** Update existing cybersecurity legislation to include quantum threats explicitly.

- **Extend EuroQCI:** Broaden the network's coverage to include critical non-governmental services.

- **Promote Crypto-Agility:** Encourage organizations to adopt flexible cryptographic systems that can quickly adapt to new algorithms.

- **Foster International Collaboration:** Lead efforts to create global standards for quantum-safe cryptography.

- **Invest in Education:** Develop programs to increase the pool of quantum cybersecurity experts in Europe.

- **Public-Private Partnerships:** Encourage government, academia, and industry collaboration to accelerate quantum-safe solutions.

Conclusion

The EU must act decisively to prepare for the quantum computing era. By leveraging its digital policy and cryptography strengths, fostering international cooperation, and supporting industry transitions, the EU can mitigate quantum cybersecurity risks while capitalizing on quantum computing's benefits. Timely action is crucial to ensure the EU's digital economy remains innovative and secure in the face of quantum advancements.

Further Reading

European Commission. "Digital Europe Programme: Quantum Technologies." 2023.

National Institute of Standards and Technology. "Post-Quantum Cryptography." 2024.

ENISA. "Post-Quantum Cryptography: Current State and Quantum Mitigation." 2021.

Mosca, M. & Piani, M. "Quantum Threat Timeline Report." Global Risk Institute, 2023.

European Parliament Research Service. "Quantum Technologies in the EU." 2022.

Six

Artificial Intelligence, Diplomacy, and Democracy: from divergence to convergence

Chris Kremidas-Courtney, Friends of Europe, March 2024

This report examines how artificial intelligence (AI) could potentially improve diplomatic processes and strengthen democratic systems. While AI offers promising capabilities for data analysis and decision support in diplomacy, its ability to directly resolve complex geopolitical issues may be limited. However, emerging AI technologies like artificial swarm intelligence (ASI) show potential for facilitating consensus-building and more inclusive democratic participation.

Key Findings

- **AI in Diplomacy:** Can assist with data analysis, language translation, and crisis monitoring. Limited in directly resolving complex geopolitical issues on its own. May struggle with uncommon situations where human judgment excels.

- **Artificial Swarm Intelligence (ASI):** Enables groups to reach consensus on divisive issues efficiently. Used successfully by UN agencies for food security assessments. Could potentially improve trade negotiations and conflict resolution.

- **Digital Democracy Initiatives:** Platforms like Taiwan's vTaiwan and Join enable citizen participation in policymaking. Brazil's Mudamos app allows citizens to propose laws. Adoption and impact of these tools remains limited in most countries.

- **Potential Benefits:** ASI shown to produce more satisfactory outcomes than traditional voting. Could make representative governments more effective. Enables inclusion of citizen stakeholders in diplomatic processes.

- **Challenges:** Overcoming political resistance to evidence-based approaches. Protecting minority opinions while achieving consensus. Scaling ASI for large-scale elections and referendums. Guarding against malign influences in online democratic processes.

Analysis

While AI shows promise in supporting diplomatic and democratic processes, its impact is likely to be evolutionary rather than revolutionary. The most significant potential lies in AI's ability to facilitate more inclusive decision-making and consensus-building, rather than in replacing human judgment. ASI and similar technologies could help address some of the polarization and gridlock issues facing modern democracies, but their implementation faces both technical and political hurdles.

Recommendations

- **Explore ASI Integration:** Governments should pilot ASI technologies for parliamentary decision-making and public consultations on specific policy issues.

- **Enhance Digital Democracy:** Expand and improve citizen participation platforms, learning from successful examples like Taiwan's vTaiwan.

- **Diplomatic Applications:** Test ASI and other AI tools in international negotiations, starting with less contentious issues.

- **Safeguard Minority Voices:** Ensure AI-enabled consensus tools do not suppress important dissenting opinions.

- **Security Measures:** Develop robust protections against manipulation of AI-enabled democratic processes.

- **Public Education:** Inform citizens about new AI-enabled participation tools to encourage adoption.

- **International Cooperation:** Share best practices and lessons learned in AI-enhanced diplomacy and democracy among nations.

Conclusion

AI technologies, particularly ASI, offer potential to evolve diplomatic and democratic processes for the digital age. While not a panacea, these tools could help address some of the challenges facing modern governance by facilitating more inclusive and satisfactory decision-making. However, careful implementation and ongoing evaluation will be crucial to realizing these benefits while safeguarding core democratic values.

Further Reading

Rosenberg, L. "Artificial Swarm Intelligence, a Human-in-the-Loop Approach to A.I." AAAI Conference on Artificial Intelligence, 2022.

Tang, A. "Digital Social Innovation to Empower Democracy." Social Media + Society, 2023.

Noveck, B.S. "Smart Citizens, Smarter State: The Technologies of Expertise and the Future of Governing." Harvard University Press, 2021.

Nemitz, P. & Remmers, M. "Artificial Intelligence and Democracy." Springer, 2022.

European Commission. "AI for Democracy: Citizen Participation and Machine Learning." 2023.

SEVEN

Is the EU Missing Another Tech Wave with AI?

Ryan Murphy, Atlantic Council, February 2024

This report examines the differences in private funding for artificial intelligence (AI) companies between the United States and European Union, as well as the regulatory approaches taken by both regions. While the US has a significant lead in AI investment, the EU is taking steps to boost its AI sector while also implementing comprehensive regulations. The analysis suggests that although regulatory approaches are converging, the funding gap remains a major challenge for EU competitiveness in AI.

Key Findings

- **AI Funding Disparities:** US companies like OpenAI have raised substantially more private capital than EU counterparts. Over 90% of venture capital for generative AI was concentrated in the US in 2023. The US has a much larger overall venture capital market compared to the EU.

- **Regulatory Approaches:** The EU has finalized its comprehensive AI Act, focusing on risk-based regulation. The US has taken a lighter regulatory approach via executive order, but with similar focus areas. Both regions are coordinating approaches through international forums like the G7.

- **EU Policy Response:** The EU is pairing regulations with incentives for AI startups. New measures include access to supercomputers and financial support targeting €4 billion by 2027.

- **Startup Ecosystem:** Nearly twice as many generative AI startups were founded in the US compared to the EU and UK combined. European startups face more competition for limited VC funding compared to US counterparts.

- **Potential Economic Impact:** Widespread AI adoption could add up to $4.4 trillion to the global economy annually. AI is increasingly seen as a critical technology for economic competitiveness and national security.

Analysis

The stark difference in private funding for AI between the US and EU presents a significant challenge for European competitiveness in this crucial technology sector. While the EU's comprehensive regulatory approach may help shape global standards, it risks stifling innovation without sufficient support for startups. The EU's recent initiatives to boost AI funding and provide resources like supercomputer access are steps in the right direction, but more is needed to close the substantial gap with the US.

The convergence of regulatory approaches between the US and EU is a positive development that could create a more unified global framework for AI governance. However, the persistence of the funding gap suggests that more than regulation is needed to hold back European AI innovation.

Recommendations

- **Expand Funding Initiatives:** The EU should consider further expanding and accelerating its financial support for AI startups to help close the funding gap with the US.

- **Foster VC Ecosystem:** Implement policies to encourage the growth of the European venture capital market, making more funding available to startups.

- **Regulatory Balance:** Ensure that AI regulations are implemented in a way that protects citizens while not overly burdening young companies.

- **International Collaboration:** Continue coordinating regulatory approaches with the US and other partners to create a cohesive global framework for AI governance.

- **Talent Retention:** Develop strategies to retain AI talent in Europe and attract international expertise to boost the EU's competitive position.

- **Public-Private Partnerships:** Encourage collaboration between government, academia, and industry to accelerate AI innovation and adoption.

Conclusion

While the EU has made strides in developing a comprehensive regulatory framework for AI and is taking steps to support its AI sector, it faces a significant challenge in competing with the US in terms of private funding and startup ecosystem. Addressing this disparity will be crucial for the EU to remain competitive in the rapidly evolving field of AI and to reap the potential economic benefits of this transformative technology.

Further Reading

European Commission. "Artificial Intelligence Act." 2023.

White House. "Executive Order on the Safe, Secure, and Trustworthy Development and Use of Artificial Intelligence." 2023.

McKinsey Global Institute. "The Economic Potential of Generative AI: The Next Productivity Frontier." 2023.

Accel. "Euroscape 2023: The State of European Tech." 2023.

Atlantic Council. "The EU-US Trade and Technology Council: Assessments and Recommendations." 2024.

EIGHT

Should the UN Govern Global AI?

Cameron F. Kerry, Joshua P. Meltzer, Andrea Renda, and Andrew W. Wyckoff, Brookings Institution, February 2024

This report examines the recent proposal from the UN AI Advisory Body for a global AI governance framework. While acknowledging the need for international cooperation on AI governance, the authors argue for a distributed and iterative approach involving multiple stakeholders rather than a single centralized UN body. The analysis highlights existing initiatives and recommends specific steps to enhance global AI governance.

Key Findings

- **UN Proposal:** The UN AI Advisory Body called for a "global governance framework" for AI. Proposed seven layers of governance functions for an institution or network of institutions.

- **Existing Initiatives:** Multiple national and international efforts already underway (e.g., OECD, Global Partnership on AI, UNESCO). Varying approaches include legislation, voluntary frameworks, and international standards.

- **Challenges:** No single initiative can address all AI governance challenges alone. Need for participation from governments, private companies, and other stakeholders. Implementing shared principles requires time and diverse use case exploration.

- **Recommended Approaches:** Scale up initiatives like the US "National AI Research Resource" internationally. Pursue joint R&D projects, especially in areas like climate change research. Support private sector initiatives to explore and mitigate AI risks. Encourage collaboration between national AI safety institutes.

- **Role of the UN:** Can convene broader group of nations than other bodies. Should not displace existing efforts, but help articulate shared vision. Focus on supporting UN Sustainable Development Goals through AI.

Analysis

The authors argue against centralizing global AI governance under a single UN body, instead advocating for a more flexible, networked approach. This position recognizes the complexity of AI governance challenges and the need for diverse perspectives and expertise. The recommendation to build on existing initiatives rather than create entirely new structures is pragmatic, potentially allowing for faster progress.

The emphasis on joint R&D projects and scaling up research resources internationally could address concerns about AI development being concentrated in a few countries or companies. However, the report needs to deeply address potential conflicts between national interests and global governance goals.

Recommendations

- **Enhance Coordination:** Develop mechanisms to better align and share information between existing AI governance initiatives.

- **Expand Research Access:** Support international expansion of AI research resources to democratize development.

- **Prioritize Use Cases:** Identify key areas (e.g., climate change) for initial focus of joint AI R&D efforts.

- **Stakeholder Engagement:** Ensure meaningful participation from diverse stakeholders in governance discussions.

- **Flexible Framework:** Design governance approaches that can adapt to rapid technological changes.

- **UN as Facilitator:** Leverage UN's convening power to articulate shared principles without centralizing all governance.

Conclusion

While the UN has an important role to play in global AI governance, a distributed and iterative approach involving multiple stakeholders is likely to be more effective than a centralized UN body. Building on existing initiatives, fostering international collaboration on research, and focusing on practical implementation of shared principles should be priorities in developing a global AI governance framework.

Further Reading

OECD. "Artificial Intelligence in Society." 2019.

Global Partnership on AI. "Working Group Reports." 2023.

UNESCO. "Recommendation on the Ethics of Artificial Intelligence." 2021.

Brookings Institution. "The Future of Global AI Governance." 2023.

European Commission. "White Paper on Artificial Intelligence - A European Approach." 2020.

NINE

Fairness in Machine Learning: regulation or standards?

Mike H. M. Teodorescu and Christos Makridis, Brookings Institution, February 2024

This report examines whether machine learning (ML) fairness should be regulated by the government or addressed through industry standards. It analyzes existing regulatory frameworks, industry standards, and the challenges of defining and implementing ML fairness. The authors recommend a combined approach of industry-led standards complemented by government regulations to effectively address ML fairness concerns.

Key Findings

- **ML Fairness Complexity:** Multiple definitions of fairness exist (e.g., demographic parity, equalized odds). Trade-offs often required between different fairness criteria. Difficult to satisfy all fairness criteria simultaneously, especially with multiple protected attributes.

- **Existing Regulatory Approaches:** Cybersecurity regulations like GDPR, HIPAA, and CCPA provide potential models. AI-specific guidelines emerging from government and industry bodies. Current regulations often lack specificity for ML fairness issues.

- **Industry Standards:** Organizations like ISO, IEEE, and NIST have developed technology standards. Standards can be more flexible and faster to develop than regulations. Certification to standards can provide market differentiation.

- **Challenges:** Lack of consumer visibility into ML fairness practices. Limited commercial incentives for companies to prioritize fairness. Complexity of fairness concepts makes consumer understanding difficult.

- **Recommendations:** Develop industry-led ML fairness standards with external auditing mechanisms. Create "bug bounty" programs for reporting fairness issues. Establish baseline regulatory requirements complemented by industry standards. Encourage innovation beyond minimum regulatory compliance

---

Analysis

The authors argue that relying solely on government regulation or industry self-regulation is insufficient to address ML fairness concerns. Regulations can provide a baseline of requirements and enforcement mechanisms, but may need more flexibility to keep pace with rapidly evolving technology. Industry standards can promote best practices and innovation, but may only be adopted with regulatory incentives.

A combined approach leverages the strengths of both regulatory and standards-based frameworks. Industry-led standards can provide technical specificity and encourage competition on fairness metrics, while government regulations can ensure a minimum level of compliance and provide recourse for affected individuals.

Recommendations

- **Develop ML Fairness Standards:** Encourage organizations like IEEE, ACM, and ISO to create comprehensive ML fairness standards.

- **External Auditing:** Implement regular external audits of ML systems for fairness compliance.

- **Fairness Bug Bounties:** Establish programs for users and researchers to report potential fairness issues in ML systems.

- **Baseline Regulations:** Create regulations mandating basic fairness criteria and transparency in algorithmic decision-making.

- **Incentivize Innovation:** Design regulatory frameworks that encourage companies to exceed minimum requirements.

- **Consumer Education:** Develop initiatives to help consumers understand ML fairness concepts and their rights.

- **Multidisciplinary Collaboration:** Ensure computer scientists, lawyers, ethicists, and business experts contribute to standards and regulations.

Conclusion

Addressing ML fairness requires a nuanced approach that combines industry-led standards with government regulation. This strategy can provide the necessary flexibility to adapt to technological changes while ensuring a baseline level of protection for individuals. As ML systems become increasingly prevalent, developing effective governance frameworks for fairness is crucial to mitigate potential harms and maintain public trust in AI technologies.

Further Reading

Mehrabi, N., et al. "A Survey on Bias and Fairness in Machine Learning." ACM Computing Surveys, 2021.

Chouldechova, A. "Fair Prediction with Disparate Impact: A Study of Bias in Recidivism Prediction Instruments." Big Data, 2017.

NIST. "AI Risk Management Framework (AI RMF 1.0)." 2023.

European Commission. "Proposal for a Regulation on Artificial Intelligence." 2021.

Kearns, M. & Roth, A. "The Ethical Algorithm: The Science of Socially Aware Algorithm Design." Oxford University Press, 2019.

Ten

Licensing AI is Not the Answer, but it Contains the Answers

Tom Wheeler, Brookings Institution, February 2024

This report analyzes recent proposals from AI industry leaders to create a licensing system for large AI models. It argues that licensing alone is insufficient and potentially problematic, but that elements of the proposals point to more effective approaches for AI governance. The analysis recommends developing comprehensive AI standards and creating a dedicated regulatory agency to oversee the AI industry.

As artificial intelligence (AI) continues to advance rapidly, prominent industry figures like OpenAI CEO Sam Altman have called for government regulation of AI, including a licensing system for large AI models. This report examines the merits and limitations of such proposals and suggests alternative approaches to effective AI governance.

Key Findings

- **Limitations of Licensing:** Licensing tends to be anti-competitive and favors incumbent companies.

Open-source AI models make licensing of only large models impractical. Historical examples like radio spectrum licensing show drawbacks of this approach. The author argues that licensing would likely stifle competition and innovation while failing to address the full scope of AI's societal impacts. The proliferation of open-source AI models further complicates the feasibility of a licensing system focused only on large-scale models.

- **Need for Broad Standards:** Standards should cover technical and behavioral aspects of AI. Focus should be on effects and outcomes rather than just capabilities. Standards must apply to all AI systems, not just large models. The report emphasizes the importance of developing comprehensive standards that address the effects and outcomes of AI systems rather than just their capabilities. These standards should apply broadly across the industry to effectively mitigate potential harms while allowing for continued innovation.

- **Regulatory Approach:** A new dedicated AI regulatory agency is needed. Agency should oversee standards development and enforcement. Multistakeholder process involving government, industry, and civil society recommended. The analysis suggests that a dedicated AI regulatory agency with appropriate expertise is necessary to oversee the rapidly evolving AI landscape effectively. This agency should facilitate a multistakeholder process to develop and enforce AI standards.

- **Challenges:** Rapidly evolving AI capabilities make standard-setting difficult. Balancing innovation with protective measures is complex. Existing regulatory structures are often insufficient for AI oversight. The report acknowledges the significant challenges in regulating AI, including the pace of technological change and the need to balance innovation with protective measures. It argues that existing regulatory frameworks often need to be revised for addressing the unique challenges posed by AI.

- **Industry Initiatives:** Tech companies have created some AI standards collaboratively. These efforts lack focus on societal impacts of AI. While recognizing industry-led efforts to develop technical standards, the report notes that these initiatives often need to adequately address broader societal concerns related to AI deployment.

Analysis

The article argues that while recent calls for AI licensing from industry leaders signal a positive shift toward accepting regulation, licensing itself is not an appropriate solution. Instead, the analysis suggests that two elements from the licensing proposals provide a stronger foundation for effective AI governance: creating comprehensive standards and establishing a dedicated regulatory agency.

By focusing on developing standards that address the effects and outcomes of AI systems rather than just their capabilities and by applying these standards broadly across the industry, regulators can better mitigate potential harms while allowing for continued innovation. The report draws parallels to other industries where effects-based standards have been successfully implemented, such as building codes and food safety regulations.

The author emphasizes the importance of a multistakeholder approach to AI governance, involving government, industry, and civil society in developing standards and policies. This collaborative process is seen as essential for creating regulations that are both effective and adaptable to rapidly changing technology.

Recommendations

- **Develop Comprehensive AI Standards:** Create technical and behavioral standards that apply to all AI systems, focusing on effects and outcomes.

- **Establish a New AI Regulatory Agency:** Create a dedicated agency with AI expertise to oversee standards development and enforcement.

- **Implement a Multistakeholder Process:** Involve government, industry, and civil society in developing AI standards and policies.

- **Focus on Near-term Impacts:** Prioritize addressing practical near-term capabilities and effects of AI rather than speculative long-term scenarios.

- **Build on Existing Laws:** Enforce existing laws against fraud, discrimination, etc., in the context of AI applications.

- **Encourage Industry Collaboration:** Support industry-led efforts to develop technical standards while addressing broader societal concerns.

- **Create Flexible Oversight Mechanisms:** Design regulatory approaches that can adapt to rapidly evolving AI capabilities.

Conclusion

While the AI industry's openness to regulation is a positive development, effective AI governance requires more than a licensing system for large models. By developing comprehensive standards for all AI systems and creating a dedicated regulatory agency, policymakers can better address the complex challenges posed by AI while fostering innovation and protecting public interests. The proposed approach aims to balance the need for oversight with the flexibility required to adapt to a rapidly evolving technological landscape.

As AI continues to transform society, governance frameworks must evolve to keep pace. The recommendations in this report provide a starting point for developing a more comprehensive and effective approach to AI regulation that goes beyond licensing to address the broader impacts of AI on individuals and society.

Further Reading

Executive Office of the President. "Executive Order on the Safe, Secure, and Trustworthy Development and Use of Artificial Intelligence." 2023.

National Institute of Standards and Technology. "AI Risk Management Framework (AI RMF 1.0)." 2023.

European Commission. "Proposal for a Regulation on Artificial Intelligence." 2021.

Cath, C. et al. "Artificial Intelligence and the 'Good Society': The US, EU, and UK Approach." Science and Engineering Ethics, 2018.

Whittaker, M. et al. "AI Now Report 2018." AI Now Institute, 2018.

Eleven

Tech Firms' Promise to Fight Election Fakes is a Good Start, But Only a Start

J. Scott Marcus, Bruegel, February 2024

This report analyzes the recent **"Tech Accord to Combat Deceptive Use of AI in 2024 Elections"** signed by 20 major technology companies. While the voluntary agreement is a positive first step, the report argues that much more urgent and coordinated action is needed to effectively mitigate the risks of AI-driven election manipulation.

Key Findings

- **Growing Threat of AI Election Manipulation:** Rapid advances in AI, especially deep fake technology, increase risks. Tense geopolitical climate provides incentives for bad actors. Multiple major elections in 2024 heighten urgency.

- **Tech Accord Overview:** Signed by 20 leading tech firms including Google, Meta, Microsoft, OpenAI. Commits to voluntary measures to combat "deceptive election content." Includes risk assessment, detection efforts, stakeholder engagement.

- **Limitations of the Accord:** Purely voluntary with no enforcement mechanism. Commitments are vague and non-specific. Not enough time to implement comprehensive solutions before 2024 elections.

- **Positive Aspects:** Represents industry acknowledgment of the problem. Encourages cooperation between competing firms. Some signatories already have relevant tools and research to build on.

- **Implementation Challenges:** Firms have varying capabilities to take concrete action. Limited time before elections constrains new technical implementations. Need for coordinated effort across many stakeholders.

Analysis

The Tech Accord represents an important first step in addressing AI-driven election manipulation, but needs to provide a comprehensive solution. The voluntary nature and lack of specific commitments limit its potential impact. However, given the threat's urgency and the problem's complexity, a non-binding agreement focused on encouraging industry cooperation and best practices is a pragmatic starting point.

The author argues that criticisms of the Accord's limitations, while valid, miss the point that perfect solutions are not currently feasible given time constraints and the rapidly evolving nature of AI technology. Instead, the focus should be on taking immediate practical steps to mitigate risks, even if incomplete.

The varying capabilities of signatory companies present both a challenge and an opportunity. While some firms may struggle to implement significant new measures quickly, others with existing resources and expertise in content moderation can likely take more substantial action in the near term.

Recommendations

- **Urgent Implementation:** Tech firms, especially those with existing capabilities, should move quickly to implement concrete measures based on the Accord.

- **Enhanced Cooperation:** Encourage increased information sharing and collaboration between signatory companies to leverage collective expertise.

- **Stakeholder Engagement:** Firms should actively engage with election officials, civil society, and other relevant stakeholders to inform their efforts.

- **Transparency:** Companies should provide clear, regular updates on their specific actions taken to combat deceptive election content.

- **Continuous Improvement:** Treat the Accord as a starting point, with ongoing efforts to strengthen commitments and develop more comprehensive solutions.

- **Public Awareness:** Support initiatives to educate voters about the risks of AI-generated disinformation and how to identify it.

- **Prepare for Future Regulation:** While voluntary measures are appropriate now, companies should anticipate and prepare for potential mandatory regulations in the future.

Conclusion

The Tech Accord to Combat Deceptive Use of AI in 2024 Elections is a positive initial step in addressing a critical threat to democratic processes. However, it must be viewed as only the beginning of a much larger, more coordinated effort. Tech companies, policymakers, and civil society must work with urgency to develop and implement more robust solutions to protect election integrity in the face of rapidly advancing AI capabilities.

Further Reading

European Commission. "Proposal for a Regulation on Artificial Intelligence." 2021.

Chesney, R. & Citron, D. "Deep Fakes: A Looming Challenge for Privacy, Democracy, and National Security." California Law Review, 2019.

Paris Call for Trust and Security in Cyberspace. "Combating Election Interference." 2023.

NATO Strategic Communications Centre of Excellence. "Digital Hydra: Security Implications of AI Generated Information Environments." 2023.

Brundage, M. et al. "The Malicious Use of Artificial Intelligence: Forecasting, Prevention, and Mitigation." 2018.

TWELVE

Intellectual Monopolization on Steroids: Big Tech in the AI age

Dr. Cecilia Rikap, Associate Professor in Economics, University College London, Friedrich Ebert Stiftung, Future of Work, February 2024

This report examines how major technology companies, particularly from the US and China, are consolidating control over artificial intelligence (AI) technologies and their associated profits. Despite widespread AI research, a small number of Big Tech firms are leveraging their resources and market position to monopolize the field's intellectual property and economic benefits.

Key Findings

- **Concentration of AI Benefits:** Despite widespread AI development, profits are captured by a few US and Chinese Big Tech companies. Europe lags behind in capitalizing on AI advancements, despite producing frontier models.

- **Intellectual Property Strategies:** Big Tech companies co-author 80-90% of their scientific publications. They share ownership of only 0.1-0.3% of their patents. This strategy allows them to benefit from open research while maintaining proprietary control.

- **Venture Capital and Start-up Control:** Major tech firms are prominent venture capital investors (e.g., Alphabet invested in 859 startups). This gives them steering power over R&D and access to emerging knowledge and talent. Example: Microsoft's multi-billion dollar backing of OpenAI since 2019.

- **Infrastructure Monopolization:** Big Tech controls key AI infrastructure like cloud computing (65% market share for Amazon, Microsoft, and Google). They monopolize code co-produced with researchers and developers. Control extends to data harvesting and compute power.

- **Technological Dependence:** Cloud services sold as "black boxes" create long-term dependence for various industries. This dependence extends from small developing companies to other leading corporations.

Analysis

The article argues that the current dynamics in AI development and commercialization reinforce existing core-periphery structures in the global economy. While AI research is conducted globally, including in Europe, the economic benefits are primarily captured by a few US and Chinese tech giants.

The author contends that this concentration of intellectual property and infrastructure control by Big Tech companies is stifling broader technological diffusion and complementary innovations. This, in turn, limits the potential for AI to drive widespread social and economic progress.

The strategies employed by Big Tech firms, such as extensive venture capital investments and control over key infrastructure like cloud computing, create a self-reinforcing cycle of dominance. These companies can maintain their technological and market advantages by steering the direction of AI research and development across the industry.

Recommendations

- Intellectual Property Reform: Reevaluate patent and copyright laws to encourage broader dissemination of AI technologies.

- Antitrust Measures: Consider stronger antitrust actions to address the concentration of power in the AI sector.

- Open Infrastructure: Promote the development of open, accessible AI infrastructure to reduce dependence on Big Tech clouds.

- Research Funding: Increase public funding for AI research with conditions that ensure wider access to results.

- Start-up Support: Develop policies to support AI start-ups in maintaining independence from Big Tech investors.

- International Cooperation: Foster collaboration between regions (e.g., EU, US, China) to prevent further entrenchment of core-periphery structures.

- Transparency Requirements: Implement regulations requiring greater transparency in AI systems and their development processes.

Conclusion

The current trajectory of AI development and commercialization risks exacerbating existing economic inequalities and technological dependencies. To realize the full potential of AI for social and economic progress, policymakers must address the extreme forms of intellectual monopoly being consolidated by Big Tech companies. This will require a multi-faceted approach involving reforms to intellectual property laws, antitrust measures, and support for more open and distributed AI development ecosystems.

Further Reading

Rikap, C. & Lundvall, B.Å. "Big tech, knowledge predation and the implications for development." Innovation and Development, 2020.

Zuboff, S. "The Age of Surveillance Capitalism." Profile Books, 2019.

OECD. "Artificial Intelligence in Society." OECD Publishing, 2019.

European Commission. "White Paper on Artificial Intelligence - A European approach to excellence and trust." 2020.

Lee, K.F. "AI Superpowers: China, Silicon Valley, and the New World Order." Houghton Mifflin Harcourt, 2018.

THIRTEEN

The AI Election Year: how to counter the impact of Artificial Intelligence

Dr. Katja Muñoz, German Council on Foreign Relations, February 2024

This report examines the growing threat of AI-enhanced influence operations on election integrity, particularly in the context of Germany and the European Union's upcoming elections in 2024. It analyzes the evolving social media landscape, the role of generative AI in amplifying disinformation, and proposes strategies for tech companies, governments, and international organizations to counter these threats.

Over 70 elections will be held worldwide in 2024, including crucial votes in Germany, the EU, and the US. This convergence of elections, along with geopolitical disruptions and rapidly advancing AI technologies, present significant challenges to democratic processes. This report outlines the current threat landscape and recommends an assertive defense strategy to protect election integrity.

Key Findings

- **Evolving Social Media Ecosystem:** Decentralization of platforms leading to user migration to smaller, niche networks. Creation of echo chambers and ideological bubbles through algorithmic curation. Shift in perceiving information as a "theater of war" rather than just a tool.

- **AI-Enhanced Influence Operations:** Generative AI supercharging existing tactics for creating synthetic content. Reduction in cost and effort to produce sophisticated disinformation. Potential for AI-powered chatbots to establish one-on-one relationships with voters.

- **Scale of Threat:** Detection of 40,000 inauthentic accounts on X (Twitter) during Israel-Hamas conflict. Discovery of 600,000 dormant inauthentic accounts on Facebook. Identification of 50,000 inauthentic accounts on X conducting disinformation in Germany.

- **Vulnerabilities in Current Defenses:** Imbalance in ability to punish perpetrators that influence campaigns. Limitations of current tech company initiatives (e.g., watermarking, content provenance). Fragmentation of social media landscape complicating coordinated responses.

Analysis

The confluence of a transforming social media landscape, advanced AI technologies, and geopolitical tensions creates a perfect storm for election interference. The decentralization of social media platforms, while offering alternatives to users, also fragments the information ecosystem and makes it harder to implement unified defense strategies.

Generative AI significantly lowers the barriers to creating convincing synthetic content, enabling more sophisticated and cost-effective influence operations. The potential for AI-powered chatbots to engage in personalized, one-on-one manipulation of voters represents a particularly concerning development that could be difficult to detect and counter.

The scale of inauthentic account networks discovered on major platforms underscores the industrial nature of modern influence operations. These coordinated efforts go beyond simple disinformation to represent sustained attempts to manipulate the overall health of the information environment.

Current defensive measures, while well-intentioned, often need to catch up due to their ease of circumvention and the rapidly evolving nature of the threat. A more comprehensive and assertive approach is needed to protect election integrity effectively.

Recommendations

For Tech Companies and Social Media Platforms:

- Implement robust identity verification systems while balancing user privacy.

- Increase barriers to account creation to deter inauthentic activities.

- Integrate digital nudging mechanisms to promote responsible engagement.

- Limit virality features like unrestricted resharing.

- Restore and enhance content moderation and trust & safety measures.

For Germany, the EU, and NATO:

- Ensure effective implementation of the Digital Services Act across Europe.

- Adopt asymmetric tactics to impose greater costs on threat actors (e.g., no-fly lists, sanctions, restricting access to Western finance).

- Enforce collaboration between tech companies, including information sharing.

- Develop innovative media literacy programs focused on recognizing synthetic content and rhetorical manipulation.

- Create contingency plans for rapid response to information vacuums during crises.

- Collaborate with social media influencers to disseminate accurate information.

International Cooperation:

- Establish repositories for sharing information on influence operations across platforms and countries.

- Develop coordinated response plans for cross-border influence campaigns.

- Harmonize regulatory approaches to create a unified front against threats.

Research and Innovation:

- Invest in advanced AI detection technologies to identify synthetic content.

- Study the psychological impacts of AI-enhanced influence operations.

- Develop ethical AI systems to counter malicious uses of the technology.

Conclusion

The integrity of elections in 2024 and beyond faces unprecedented challenges from AI-enhanced influence operations. While the threats are significant, Germany, the EU, and their allies are not defenseless. By implementing a comprehensive, assertive defense strategy that combines technological innovation, regulatory action, international cooperation, and public education, democracies can work to safeguard the integrity of their information spaces and electoral processes.

The battle for information integrity is ongoing and requires sustained effort and adaptation. As AI technologies continue to advance, so too must our defenses. Protecting democratic discourse and decision-making in the AI age will require unprecedented collaboration between governments, tech companies, civil society, and citizens.

Further Reading

European External Action Service. "Foreign Information Manipulation and Interference Threats." 2023.

Bradshaw, S. & Howard, P.N. "The Global Disinformation Order: 2019 Global Inventory of Organised Social Media Manipulation." Oxford Internet Institute, 2019.

Woolley, S.C. & Howard, P.N. "Computational Propaganda: Political Parties, Politicians, and Political Manipulation on Social Media." Oxford University Press, 2018.

NATO Strategic Communications Centre of Excellence. "Robotrolling." Quarterly reports.

Chesney, R. & Citron, D. "Deep Fakes: A Looming Challenge for Privacy, Democracy, and National Security." California Law Review, 2019.

FOURTEEN

Artificial Intelligence and Democracy

Armin Grunwald, Michael Hirschbrich, Viktor Mayer-Schonberger,
Haralad Leitenmuller, Bettina Rausch, Julia Reuss

Wilfried Martens Centre for European Studies

This report examines the impact of artificial intelligence (AI) on democracy, focusing on the challenges and opportunities presented by this rapidly evolving technology. As AI continues to advance, it has the potential to significantly influence democratic processes, from election integrity to citizen participation and governance. This analysis explores key areas where AI intersects with democracy, highlighting both the promising applications and potential risks. The report aims to provide policymakers and stakeholders with a comprehensive understanding of the current landscape and offer recommendations for harnessing AI's potential while safeguarding democratic principles.

Key Findings

- AI technologies have the potential to both enhance and undermine democratic processes, depending on how they are developed and deployed.

- The spread of AI-generated disinformation and deepfakes poses a significant threat to informed democratic discourse and election integrity.

- AI-driven personalization in social media and news consumption can create echo chambers and filter bubbles, potentially polarizing public opinion.

- AI systems can improve government efficiency and transparency, but their use in decision-making raises concerns about accountability and bias.

- The development of AI governance frameworks and digital literacy initiatives is crucial for maintaining democratic values in the AI era.

Analysis

The integration of AI into various aspects of society presents both opportunities and challenges for democratic systems. On one hand, AI has the potential to enhance democratic participation by improving access to information, streamlining government services, and enabling more efficient decision-making processes. For instance, AI-powered chatbots and virtual assistants can provide citizens with instant access to government information and services, increasing engagement and transparency.

However, the same technologies that can bolster democracy also have the potential to undermine it. One of the most pressing concerns is the proliferation of AI-generated disinformation and deepfakes. These sophisticated technologies can create highly convincing false content, making it increasingly difficult for citizens to distinguish fact from fiction. This poses a significant threat to informed democratic discourse and the integrity of elections. As AI-generated content becomes more prevalent and convincing, there is a risk of eroding public trust in information sources and democratic institutions.

Another critical area of concern is the impact of AI on information consumption and public discourse. AI-driven algorithms used by social media platforms and news aggregators often prioritize engagement over diversity of viewpoints. This can lead to the creation of echo chambers and filter bubbles, where individuals are primarily exposed to information that confirms their existing beliefs. The resulting polarization can hinder constructive dialogue and compromise, which are essential elements of a healthy democracy.

The use of AI in government decision-making processes also raises important questions about accountability and transparency. While AI systems can process vast amounts of data to inform policy decisions, their complexity often makes it difficult for the public to understand how these decisions are reached. This "black box" nature of AI algorithms can undermine the principle of democratic accountability and potentially introduce biases that disproportionately affect certain groups.

On the positive side, AI has the potential to significantly improve government efficiency and responsiveness. Predictive analytics can help governments anticipate and address public needs more effectively. AI-powered systems can also enhance the detection of fraud and corruption, contributing to more transparent and accountable governance.

The development of AI is also raising new questions about digital rights and privacy. As AI systems become more sophisticated in processing personal data, there is a growing need to establish robust frameworks for data protection and ethical AI use. Balancing the benefits of data-driven governance with individual privacy rights will be a key challenge for democratic societies in the coming years.

Recommendations

- Develop comprehensive AI governance frameworks that prioritize transparency, accountability, and the protection of democratic values.

- Invest in digital literacy programs to educate citizens about AI, its potential impacts, and how to critically evaluate information in the digital age.

- Implement stricter regulations and technical solutions to combat AI-generated disinformation and deepfakes, particularly in the context of elections.

- Encourage the development of AI systems that promote diverse viewpoints and cross-ideological engagement to counteract echo chambers and polarization.

- Establish clear guidelines for the use of AI in government decision-making, ensuring human oversight and the ability to explain AI-driven outcomes.

- Foster international cooperation on AI governance to address global challenges and ensure that AI development aligns with democratic principles worldwide.

Conclusion

The relationship between AI and democracy is complex and multifaceted. While AI offers significant opportunities to enhance democratic processes and governance, it also presents substantial risks that must be carefully managed. As AI continues to evolve, it is crucial for policymakers, technologists, and citizens to work together to shape its development in a way that strengthens rather than undermines democratic values. By implementing thoughtful regulations, investing in education, and fostering transparent and accountable AI systems, we can harness the potential of this powerful technology while safeguarding the foundations of democratic societies.

Further Reading

- Nemitz, P. (2018). Constitutional democracy and technology in the age of artificial intelligence. Philosophical Transactions of the Royal Society A: Mathematical, Physical and Engineering Sciences.

- Helbing, D., et al. (2019). Will Democracy Survive Big Data and Artificial Intelligence? In Towards Digital Enlightenment. Springer, Cham.

- Danaher, J., et al. (2017). Algorithmic governance: Developing a research agenda through the power of collective intelligence. Big Data & Society.

- Mittelstadt, B.D., et al. (2016). The ethics of algorithms: Mapping the debate. Big Data & Society.

- Zuboff, S. (2019). The Age of Surveillance Capitalism: The Fight for a Human Future at the New Frontier of Power. Public Affairs.

FIFTEEN

Why Artificial General Intelligence Lies Beyond Deep Learning

*Swaptik Chowdhury and Steven W. Popper, Rand Corporation,
February 2024*

This report analyzes the limitations of deep learning in achieving artificial general intelligence (AGI) and proposes alternative approaches, particularly decision-making under deep uncertainty (DMDU) methods. It argues that while deep learning has driven significant advances in AI, its fundamental approach may be unsuitable for realizing human-like general intelligence. The report recommends a shift towards more robust, decision-driven AI methods to handle real-world uncertainties and advance towards AGI.

Introduction:

Recent developments in AI, particularly in deep learning, have renewed interest in the possibility of achieving artificial general intelligence (AGI). However, this report argues that current AI approaches, primarily based on deep learning, face significant limitations in realizing AGI. It examines these limitations and proposes alternative frameworks that may offer a more promising path towards human-like artificial intelligence.

Key Findings

- **Limitations of Deep Learning:** Requires large datasets and expensive computational resources. Focuses on deriving statistical rules from training data. Struggles with uncertainty and novel situations. Follows a predictive logic that may not reflect human-like reasoning.

- **Human vs. AI Decision-Making:** Humans rely on existing representations and modify rules as needed. AI systems often lack the ability to repurpose existing knowledge flexibly. Human decision-making focuses on characterizing alternative actions rather than just predicting outcomes.

- **The "What If" Conundrum:** AGI may require enhancing inductive reasoning capabilities. Current AI struggles with hypothetical scenarios and robust decision-making.

- **Decision-Making Under Deep Uncertainty (DMDU):** DMDU methods analyze vulnerability of decisions across various future scenarios. Focus on robustness rather than optimized solutions. May provide a conceptual framework for AGI reasoning.

- **Autonomous Vehicle Example:** Current deep learning approaches struggle with unpredictable real-world conditions. DMDU methods could enhance AV performance by focusing on evaluating limited decisions rather than perfect predictions.

Analysis

The article argues that the current deep learning paradigm, while successful in many applications, needs to be revised in its ability to achieve AGI. Deep learning's reliance on statistical rules derived from large datasets makes it vulnerable to uncertainty and novel situations. This approach differs significantly from human cognition, which flexibly applies and modifies existing knowledge to new contexts.

The authors propose that achieving AGI may require a shift from predictive deductions to enhancing inductive "what if" reasoning. This shift aligns more closely with human decision-making processes, which often focus on characterizing alternative actions with respect to desired outcomes rather than simply predicting the future.

The report suggests that Decision-Making Under Deep Uncertainty (DMDU) methods could provide a valuable conceptual framework for developing AI systems capable of navigating real-world uncertainties. DMDU approaches prioritize robustness over optimality, seeking decisions that perform well across diverse future scenarios. This aligns more closely with human decision-making in complex, uncertain environments.

The autonomous vehicle example illustrates the potential benefits of this approach. By adopting a robust decision framework, AVs could handle unpredictable situations more effectively than current deep learning models, which struggle when encountering scenarios not present in their training data.

Recommendations

- **Shift Research Focus:** Encourage AI research that explores alternatives to deep learning, particularly approaches that emphasize robust decision-making in uncertain environments.

- **Invest in DMDU Methods:** Allocate resources to develop and refine Decision-Making Under Deep Uncertainty techniques for AI applications.

- **Emphasize Context-Aware AI:** Develop AI systems that can better understand and adapt to decision contexts, rather than relying solely on statistical patterns.

- **Cross-Disciplinary Collaboration:** Foster collaboration between AI researchers, cognitive scientists, and decision theorists to develop more human-like AI reasoning capabilities.

- **Real-World Testing:** Implement more rigorous testing of AI systems in complex, unpredictable environments to identify limitations and areas for improvement.

- **Ethical Considerations:** As AI systems become more capable of complex decision-making, ensure robust ethical frameworks are in place to guide their development and deployment.

Conclusion

While deep learning has driven remarkable advances in AI, there may be more suitable approaches for achieving artificial general intelligence. The path to AGI likely requires a paradigm shift towards more robust, decision-driven AI methods capable of handling real-world uncertainties. By embracing alternative frameworks like Decision-Making Under Deep Uncertainty, researchers may be able to develop AI systems that more closely emulate human-like general intelligence.

Further Reading

Popper, S.W. et al. "Robust Decision Making: Coping with Uncertainty." The RAND Journal of Economics, 2019.

Lake, B.M. et al. "Building Machines That Learn and Think Like People." Behavioral and Brain Sciences, 2017.

Marcus, G. "The Next Decade in AI: Four Steps Towards Robust Artificial Intelligence." arXiv preprint, 2020.

Lempert, R.J. et al. "Deep Uncertainty." Annual Review of Environment and Resources, 2013.

Hassabis, D. et al. "Neuroscience-Inspired Artificial Intelligence." Neuron, 2017.

SIXTEEN

The Dark Side of Urban Artificial Intelligence: addressing the environmental and social impact of algorithms

Marta Galceran-Vercher, research fellow, Global Cities Programme, CIDOB Alexandra Vidal, researcher and project manager, Global Cities Programme, CIDOB, Barcelona Centre for International Affairs, January 2024

This report analyzes trends in urban artificial intelligence (AI) initiatives based on data from the Global Observatory of Urban Artificial Intelligence's (GOUAI) Atlas of Urban AI. The Atlas compiles over 200 ethically-aligned AI projects from 70 cities worldwide. Key findings include the concentration of initiatives in Europe and North America, a focus on governance applications, an emphasis on transparency and privacy principles, and a growing trend of cities implementing AI governance policies.

Key Findings

- **Geographic Distribution:** 80% of initiatives are in North America and Europe. 10% in Asia, 8% in Latin America/Caribbean, 1% in MENA region.

Potential bias due to data collection limitations and communication disparities.

- **Sectoral Focus:** Governance and urban services dominate (66% of initiatives). Followed by mobility (24%), social services (22%), environment/resources (22%). Underrepresentation in economy/business (4%) and security/resilience (9%).

- **Ethical Principles:** Transparency/openness most common (67% of initiatives). Privacy protection second (50%). Fairness/non-discrimination (42%), safety/cybersecurity (40%), accountability (33%). Sustainability least common (6%).

- **Implementation Timeline:** 64% of initiatives started between 2017-2023. 2021 marked increased focus on local AI governance strategies.

- **Project Maturity:** 66% of initiatives fully implemented. 17% in implementation phase, 17% in planning phase.

- **Stakeholder Collaboration:** Majority involve public-private partnerships. Growing trend of city-to-city collaboration. 66% of cities in Atlas are small to medium-sized (250,000 to 1 million residents).

- **AI Governance:** 82% of initiatives are specific AI-enabled services/solutions. Only 12% are policies and 6% are strategies. 11% of cities have AI strategies/action plans. 21% have local AI governance policies/regulations.

Analysis

The Atlas reveals a significant concentration of urban AI initiatives in Europe and North America, potentially reflecting resource disparities and data collection challenges. While this may indicate leadership in ethical AI development, it also highlights the need for more inclusive global representation in future research.

Governance and urban services emerge as the primary focus for AI applications, suggesting local governments prioritize improving internal processes and citizen services. The underrepresentation of economic and security applications may reflect ethical concerns or data limitations.

Transparency and privacy protection stand out as the most commonly upheld ethical principles, likely influenced by existing regulatory frameworks like GDPR. However, the low adoption of sustainability principles indicates a critical gap in addressing AI's environmental impacts.

The rapid growth of urban AI initiatives since 2017 and the high percentage of fully implemented projects demonstrate that this technology is becoming mainstream in urban governance. However, there is a notable mismatch between AI adoption and governance frameworks, with relatively few cities having comprehensive AI strategies or policies in place.

Recommendations

- **Global Inclusivity:** Expand data collection efforts to ensure better representation of urban AI initiatives from the Global South.

- **Sustainability Focus:** Encourage cities to incorporate sustainability principles in AI projects and develop guidelines for environmentally responsible AI.

- **Governance Frameworks:** Support cities in developing comprehensive AI strategies and governance policies to match the pace of AI adoption.

- **Ethical Auditing:** Promote the use of external audits and transparency measures to ensure adherence to ethical principles, particularly for high-risk applications.

- **Knowledge Sharing:** Facilitate city-to-city collaboration and knowledge exchange on ethical AI implementation and governance best practices.

- **Capacity Building:** Develop resources to help small and medium-sized cities implement ethical AI initiatives and governance frameworks.

- **Sectoral Diversity:** Encourage exploration of ethical AI applications in underrepresented sectors like economy/business while maintaining ethical safeguards.

Conclusion

The GOUAI Atlas of Urban AI provides valuable insights into the global landscape of ethical urban AI initiatives. While significant progress has been made in implementing AI for urban governance and services, there is a pressing need for more comprehensive AI governance frameworks at the local level. As AI technology continues to evolve rapidly, cities must work to close the gap between adoption and regulation to ensure the ethical and responsible use of AI in urban environments.

Further Reading

Cugurullo, F., et al. (2023) "The rise of AI urbanism in post-smart cities: A critical commentary on urban artificial intelligence." Urban Studies.

Galceran-Vercher, M. and Rodríguez-Perez, A. (2024) "The dark side of urban Artificial Intelligence: addressing the environmental and social impact of algorithms". CIDOB Briefings, 55.

Luusua, A., et al. (2023) "Understanding the emerging role of artificial intelligence in smart cities," AI Soc., 38(3), pp. 1039-1044.

Popelka, S. et al. (2023) Urban AI Guide 202Urban AI.

European Commission. "Proposal for a Regulation on Artificial Intelligence." 2021.

The Impact of Generative AI in a Global Election Year

Valerie Wirtschafter, Brookings Institution, January 2024

This report examines the potential influence of generative artificial intelligence (AI) on democratic processes during a historic global election year in 2024. While generative AI has not yet transformed the information landscape to the degree initially anticipated, even limited use of AI-generated content poses threats to electoral integrity and democratic discourse. The report analyzes recent cases where generative AI has impacted elections, outlines potential future threats, and recommends multi-faceted strategies to address these challenges.

Key Findings

- **Current Impact of Generative AI:** Generated content makes up a small fraction of the overall contested information space. About 1% of fact-checked claims and content flagged on social media reference AI-related terms. Generated content complements existing methods of spreading false claims rather than replacing them.

- **Recent Cases of AI Impact on Elections:** Slovakia: AI-generated audio clip spread misinformation days before 2023 parliamentary election. Argentina: Potential AI audio recording influenced 2023 presidential election discourse.

- **Potential Future Threats:** Manufacturing consensus on political issues. Undermining government responsiveness. Swaying public opinion and exacerbating divisions. Demobilizing or deceiving voters. Undermining trust in electoral processes.

- **Amplification of Existing Challenges:** Easier creation of high-quality, distinct content at scale. More convincing fake social media profiles and personas. Generation of credible-seeming text in multiple languages. Creation of realistic deepfake audio and video.

- **Broader Information Ecosystem Concerns:** Fragmentation of social media platforms. Varying content moderation practices. Limited researcher access to platform data.

Analysis

The report argues that while generative AI has not yet dramatically altered the information landscape, it poses significant risks to electoral integrity and democratic discourse. Even limited use of AI-generated content can have outsized impacts, as seen in recent elections in Slovakia and Argentina. The technology amplifies existing disinformation tactics by making it easier to create convincing fake content at scale.

The authors emphasize that generative AI is just one factor in a complex information ecosystem. Other challenges include the fragmentation of social media platforms, inconsistent content moderation practices, and limited data access for researchers. These issues make it difficult to fully understand and address the impact of AI-generated content on elections.

Recommendations

The report proposes a multi-faceted approach to address the challenges posed by generative AI in elections:

Development:

- Implement watermarking and content provenance for AI-generated outputs.

- Legislate limits on generated content depicting political candidates.

- Require additional user validation for generating content featuring candidates.

Distribution:

- Close loopholes in platform policies on manipulated media.

- Enhance cross-platform collaboration to identify and limit spread of harmful content.

- Create shared databases of known generated political content.

Detection:

- Invest in improving AI detection tools.

- Expand researcher access to social media data.

- Launch widespread digital literacy education efforts.

Broader Considerations:

- Focus on harms of outputs rather than blanket restrictions on AI-generated content.

- Recognize potential beneficial uses of AI in elections (e.g., translation, increased accessibility).

- Ensure interventions do not inadvertently amplify the "liar's dividend" phenomenon.

Conclusion

While generative AI poses significant challenges to electoral integrity, a coordinated response involving tech companies, policymakers, researchers, and voters can help mitigate these risks. The report emphasizes that while no single intervention will solve the problem, a combination of technical solutions, policy changes, enhanced collaboration, and public education can make meaningful progress in safeguarding democratic processes in the AI era.

Further Reading

Chesney, R. & Citron, D. "Deep Fakes: A Looming Challenge for Privacy, Democracy, and National Security." California Law Review, 2019.

European Commission. "Proposal for a Regulation on Artificial Intelligence." 2021.

Woolley, S.C. & Howard, P.N. "Computational Propaganda: Political Parties, Politicians, and Political Manipulation on Social Media." Oxford University Press, 2018.

Paris Call for Trust and Security in Cyberspace. "Combating Election Interference." 2023.

NATO Strategic Communications Centre of Excellence. "Digital Hydra: Security Implications of AI Generated Information Environments." 2023.

EIGHTEEN

Effective AI Regulation Requires Understanding General-Purpose AI

Aylin Caliskan and Kristian Lum, Brookings Institution, January 2024

This report examines the unique challenges posed by regulating general-purpose AI models like GPT-4, which can be used for a wide variety of tasks, unlike previous machine learning models. The authors argue that effective regulation and evaluation of these models require better information about how they are actually being used in practice. Without this data, researchers and policymakers are left speculating about hypothetical risks rather than addressing concrete issues.

Key Findings

- **Differences from Traditional ML Models:**
  Previous models had specific, predictable use cases. General-purpose AI can be used for many diverse tasks. Range of potential uses is currently unknown to the public.

- **Challenges for Evaluation and Regulation:**
  Difficult to anticipate all potential risks and harms.

Context-specific issues are harder to identify and address. Existing evaluation techniques may not apply to all use cases.

- **Limited Information on Real-World Usage:** Researchers lack comprehensive data on how models are being used. Tech companies have access to usage logs but don't share widely. Government mandates only cover certain regulated industries.

- **Importance of Use Case Data:** Critical for designing targeted evaluations. Necessary to prioritize regulatory efforts. Helps identify concrete risks rather than hypothetical ones.

Analysis

The authors argue that the general-purpose nature of modern AI models like GPT-4 creates unique challenges for regulation and evaluation. Unlike previous machine learning models with specific, predictable uses, these new models can be applied to a vast array of tasks, many of which may not be anticipated by their creators or regulators.

This flexibility makes it difficult to evaluate the models for potential harms or biases, as the context of use plays a crucial role in determining the risks. Without comprehensive information on how the models are actually being used in practice, researchers and policymakers are left to speculate about hypothetical risks rather than address concrete issues.

The report emphasizes that while some information on AI use cases is available through government mandates and independent research, the most comprehensive data is held by the tech companies developing these models. The authors argue that if these companies genuinely want effective regulation, they need to be more transparent about how their models are being used in the real world.

Recommendations

- **Expand Government Reporting Mandates:** Extend requirements for reporting AI use cases beyond financial services and government agencies to other highly regulated industries.

- **Increase Independent Research:** Conduct more surveys and user interviews to gather information on AI use cases, while acknowledging limitations in capturing certain types of use.

- **Tech Company Transparency:** Encourage or require AI companies to process and share aggregated, anonymized data on how their models are being used.

- **Develop New Evaluation Techniques:** Create methods for assessing general-purpose AI models that can account for diverse and evolving use cases.

- **Prioritize High-Risk Applications:** Use information on real-world usage to focus regulatory efforts on the most impactful or immediately risky applications.

- **Foster Collaboration:** Promote information sharing between tech companies, researchers, and regulators to develop a comprehensive understanding of AI use and risks.

Conclusion

Effective regulation of general-purpose AI models requires a solid understanding of how they are actually being used in practice. While government mandates and independent research can provide some insights, tech companies developing these models have the most comprehensive data on usage. If the AI industry truly wants effective regulation, as many companies claim, they must be willing to share more information about real-world use cases. This will enable researchers and policymakers to move beyond hypothetical risks and address the concrete challenges posed by general-purpose AI in various contexts.

Further Reading

National Institute of Standards and Technology. "AI Risk Management Framework (AI RMF 1.0)." 2023.

European Commission. "Proposal for a Regulation on Artificial Intelligence." 2021.

Buolamwini, J. & Gebru, T. "Gender Shades: Intersectional Accuracy Disparities in Commercial Gender Classification." Proceedings of Machine Learning Research, 2018.

Caliskan, A., Bryson, J.J., & Narayanan, A. "Semantics derived automatically from language corpora contain human-like biases." Science, 2017.

Mitchell, M. et al. "Model Cards for Model Reporting." Proceedings of the Conference on Fairness, Accountability, and Transparency, 2019.

NINETEEN

The Implications of the AI boom for Non-State Armed Actors

Valerie Wirtschafter, Brookings Institution, January 2024

This report examines how advances in artificial intelligence (AI), particularly generative AI, could be exploited by criminal organizations, terrorist groups, and other nonstate armed actors in 2024. It analyzes potential misuses in disinformation, recruitment, intelligence gathering, and cybercrimes, while also considering how law enforcement can leverage AI to combat these threats. The report concludes with policy recommendations for mitigating risks at both national and international levels.

Key Findings

- **Information Space and Generative AI:** AI could bolster disinformation, recruitment, and intelligence efforts. Generated content could create convincing propaganda or "evidence" for extremist justification. Large language models could be used to mine information for tactical guidance.

- **Cybercrimes and Generative AI:** AI lowers technical threshold for cyber espionage and attacks. Enables more convincing spearphishing campaigns and voice cloning for fraud. Could facilitate attacks on critical infrastructure.

- **Open-Source vs. Proprietary AI:** Open-source models allow for malicious adaptations (e.g., WormGPT, FraudGPT). Proprietary models have some safeguards, but workarounds exist.

- **Law Enforcement Applications:** AI tools could help detect fraudulent activity and expose criminal networks. Proper oversight needed to ensure responsible usage by security personnel.

Analysis

The report argues that while AI offers significant benefits, its rapid advancement also creates new opportunities for malicious actors. Nonstate armed groups, which have traditionally lacked sophisticated cyber capabilities, may now be able to leverage AI to enhance their operations across multiple domains.

The accessibility of generative AI tools lowers barriers for creating convincing disinformation, personalizing recruitment efforts, and gathering intelligence. In the cyber realm, AI could enable more sophisticated and scalable attacks, potentially bringing critical infrastructure within reach of groups that previously lacked such capabilities.

The authors highlight the double-edged nature of open-source AI models. While openness can foster innovation and security improvements, it also allows for harmful adaptations. This creates a challenge for policymakers in balancing the benefits of open collaboration with the need to mitigate risks.

The report also notes that AI can be a powerful tool for law enforcement and military personnel in combating these threats. However, it emphasizes the need for responsible deployment and international cooperation to ensure these tools are not misused, particularly in contexts with weak governance.

Recommendations

- **Legislative Focus:** Develop laws that address harms of AI systems beyond just model size, incorporating auditing processes for open-source models.

- **International Cooperation:** Work towards consensus on AI governance standards, particularly with nations that have divergent norms.

- **Law Enforcement Capabilities:** Invest in AI tools for detecting fraudulent activity, exposing criminal networks, and identifying threats.

- **Responsible Deployment:** Ensure AI systems used by security personnel respect human rights and maintain human control in decision-making.

- Oversight Mechanisms: Implement proper oversight and binding contracts when collaborating with local security agencies, especially in high-corruption contexts.

- **Continuous Assessment:** Regularly audit AI systems post-release to identify and address emerging risks.

- **Research Support:** Encourage development of AI tools for cybersecurity, vulnerability patching, and other defensive applications.

Conclusion

The AI boom presents both opportunities and challenges in the realm of security and nonstate armed actors. While these technologies can amplify threats, they also offer new tools for combating malicious activities. Effective mitigation will require a multifaceted approach involving legislative action, international cooperation, and responsible development and deployment of AI systems. As the landscape continues to evolve rapidly, policymakers and security professionals must remain vigilant and adaptive in their approaches to AI governance and utilization.

Further Reading

Brundage, M. et al. "The Malicious Use of Artificial Intelligence: Forecasting, Prevention, and Mitigation." 2018.

Horowitz, M.C. et al. "Artificial Intelligence and International Security." Center for a New American Security, 2018.

Buchanan, B. "The Cybersecurity Dilemma: Hacking, Trust and Fear Between Nations." Oxford University Press, 2017.

European Union Agency for Cybersecurity. "Artificial Intelligence Cybersecurity Challenges." 2023.

National Security Commission on Artificial Intelligence. "Final Report." 2021.

TWENTY

How the EU can Navigate the Geopolitics of AI

Raluca Csernatoni, Carnegie Europe, January 2024

This report analyzes the European Union's position in the global competition for AI supremacy and governance. It examines the challenges the EU faces in promoting responsible AI development while competing with the United States and China, and proposes strategies for the EU to shape global AI governance while fostering innovation.

Key Findings

- **Global AI Competition:** US and China dominate in AI capabilities and investment. EU emphasizes responsible governance and ethical principles. Concerns about an "AI arms race" compromising safety and ethics.

- **Regulatory Landscape:** Proliferation of initiatives, principles, and voluntary codes. EU's AI Act aims to set global standard for binding regulation. Challenges in extending "Brussels effect" to AI governance.

- **EU's Challenges:** Coordinating actions across institutions and member states. Crafting cohesive European AI foreign policy. Addressing innovation lag compared to US and China.

- **Recent EU Initiatives:** AI innovation package to boost European ecosystem. Plans for "AI Factories" with dedicated supercomputers and talent. Establishment of AI Office within European Commission.

- **Geopolitical Implications:** AI impacting international relations and power dynamics. Concerns about corporate hegemony and compute power concentration. Intersection of civilian AI innovation and national security strategies.

Analysis

The EU faces a significant challenge in balancing its commitment to responsible AI development with the need to remain competitive in a rapidly evolving global landscape. While the United States and China lead in AI capabilities and investment, the EU has positioned itself as a champion of ethical and human-centric AI governance.

The EU's AI Act represents a bold attempt to set a global standard for AI regulation. However, the Union's ability to extend its regulatory influence beyond its borders (the "Brussels effect") may be limited in the AI domain due to the technology's rapid evolution and the diverse approaches taken by other major players.

The report highlights the EU's recent initiatives to boost its AI innovation ecosystem, including the AI innovation package and plans for "AI Factories." These efforts aim to address the innovation gap between the EU and its competitors while maintaining a focus on trustworthy AI development.

A key challenge for the EU will be coordinating actions across its institutions and member states to present a unified approach to AI governance and foreign policy. This is particularly important as the EU navigates relationships with the United States and China, balancing cooperation and competition.

Recommendations

- **Unified Strategy:** Develop a cohesive European AI foreign policy that aligns innovation goals with ethical principles.

- **Strategic Partnerships:** Foster alliances with key global partners to promote responsible AI governance internationally.

- **Effective Implementation:** Ensure smooth operationalization of the AI Act and establish robust oversight mechanisms.

- **Innovation Support:** Continue and expand initiatives to boost the European AI ecosystem, particularly for startups and cross-border collaboration.

- **Global Engagement:** Actively participate in shaping international AI governance frameworks while promoting EU values.

- **Talent Development:** Invest in education and training programs to build a skilled AI workforce within the EU.

- **Regulatory Flexibility:** Maintain adaptability in regulatory approaches to keep pace with rapid technological advancements.

- **Public-Private Collaboration:** Encourage partnerships between government, industry, and academia to drive responsible AI innovation.

Conclusion

The EU stands at a critical juncture in the global AI landscape. While it faces significant challenges in competing with the United States and China in terms of pure innovation and investment, the EU has an opportunity to lead in shaping responsible AI governance. Success will depend on the EU's ability to foster a competitive AI ecosystem while staying true to its values-based approach. By effectively navigating the geopolitics of AI, the EU can play a crucial role in ensuring that the technology's development aligns with democratic principles and ethical considerations on a global scale.

Further Reading

European Commission. "White Paper on Artificial Intelligence - A European approach to excellence and trust." 2020.

Brattberg, E., Csernatoni, R., & Rugge, F. "Europe and AI: Leading, Lagging Behind, or Carving Its Own Way?" Carnegie Endowment for International Peace, 2020.

Craglia, M. et al. "Artificial Intelligence: A European Perspective." Joint Research Centre, European Commission, 2018.

Roberts, H. et al. "The Chinese approach to artificial intelligence: an analysis of policy, ethics, and regulation." AI & Society, 2021.

Feijóo, C. et al. "The industrial innovation ecosystem of artificial intelligence in China: Current status and issues." AI & Society, 2020.

TWENTY ONE

Rethinking Concerns About AI's Energy Use

Daniel Castro, Center for Data Innovation, January 2024

This report examines recent claims about artificial intelligence (AI) systems' energy consumption and environmental impact. As AI adoption accelerates, some have speculated that increasing the use of large AI models could lead to massive growth in energy usage. However, many early estimates have proven to be inflated or misleading. This analysis aims to provide senior managers with an accurate understanding of AI's current and projected energy footprint, address common misconceptions, and offer recommendations for policymakers to address legitimate concerns while avoiding unintended consequences.

Key Findings

- Early predictions about digital technologies' energy use have often been wildly inaccurate, with actual consumption far lower than projected.

- Recent claims about AI systems' massive energy requirements are similarly inflated and based on flawed assumptions.

- While AI energy use will grow, increases are likely to be modest and offset by efficiency gains and environmental benefits from AI applications.

Analysis

Historical Context of Technology Energy Concerns

Concerns about the energy consumption of digital technologies are not new. During the dot-com boom of the late 1990s, alarmist predictions suggested the digital economy would soon consume half of the U.S. electric grid. These estimates proved to be wildly inaccurate. Current data from the International Energy Agency shows that data centers and data transmission networks each account for only about 1-1.5% of global electricity use.

This pattern of overestimating technology's energy impact has repeated itself multiple times:

- **Late 1990s:** Claims that half the electric grid would power the digital economy within a decade

- **2019:** Reports that 30 minutes of Netflix streaming produced emissions equivalent to driving 4 miles

In both cases, the estimates were later debunked as being based on flawed assumptions and calculation errors. The

Netflix estimate was off by two orders of magnitude - the actual impact was closer to driving 10-100 yards.

Current AI Energy Use Claims

With the recent surge of interest in AI, we are seeing a new wave of speculation about potentially massive increases in energy consumption. Critics argue that the rapid adoption of AI, combined with growth in the size of deep learning models, could lead to devastating environmental consequences.

However, as with past technologies, many early claims about AI energy use have already proven to be inflated and misleading. While exact figures are still being studied, several factors suggest the energy impact will be far more modest than alarmist predictions:

- **Efficiency improvements:** AI hardware and software are rapidly becoming more energy efficient, offsetting some of the increased usage.

- **Workload optimization:** Companies have strong incentives to optimize AI workloads to minimize costs, naturally limiting energy waste.

- **Renewable energy adoption:** Major tech companies are increasingly powering data centers with renewable energy, reducing emissions impact.

- **Beneficial applications:** Many AI applications, like smart grid management and industrial optimization, provide net positive environmental benefits.

Relative scale: Even with growth, AI energy use is likely to remain a small fraction of total global energy consumption.

Contextualizing AI Energy Use

To properly assess AI's energy impact, it's crucial to consider it in the broader context of global energy use and technology trends:

- Total data center energy use has remained relatively flat despite exponential growth in computing, due to efficiency gains.

- The tech sector has been a leader in renewable energy adoption, often exceeding national averages.

- AI-driven optimizations in areas like manufacturing, logistics, and building management can provide energy savings that offset AI's direct consumption.

While vigilance about energy use is warranted, the evidence suggests AI's impact will be manageable and potentially net positive when considering its applications in energy efficiency and environmental protection.

Recommendations

- **Develop energy transparency standards for AI models:** Encourage or require reporting of energy consumption for training and inference of large AI models to enable accurate tracking and informed decision-making.

- **Seek voluntary commitments on energy transparency for foundation models:** Work with leading AI companies to establish best practices for energy use disclosure and efficiency improvements.

- **Consider the unintended consequences of AI regulations on energy use:** Ensure that well-intentioned regulations don't inadvertently increase energy consumption by mandating inefficient practices or stifling innovation in energy-efficient AI.

- **Use AI to decarbonize government operations:** Lead by example by adopting AI solutions that improve energy efficiency in public sector operations.

Conclusion

The history of digital technology shows a clear pattern of overestimating energy consumption impacts. While AI's rapid growth warrants attention to its energy use, current evidence suggests that concerns about massive, uncontrolled increases in consumption are largely unfounded.

Efficiency improvements, renewable energy adoption, and beneficial AI applications are likely to offset much of the increased energy demand. However, proactive measures to encourage transparency and efficiency can help ensure AI development remains environmentally sustainable.

By learning from past misconceptions about technology energy use and taking a measured, evidence-based approach, policymakers and business leaders can harness AI's potential while managing its energy impact responsibly. This balanced strategy will be crucial for realizing the economic and societal benefits of AI while minimizing environmental concerns.

Further Reading

Masanet, E., et al. (2020). "Recalibrating global data center energy-use estimates." Science, 367(6481), 984-986.

Koomey, J., & Masanet, E. (2021). "Does not compute: Avoiding pitfalls assessing the Internet's energy and carbon impacts." Joule, 5(7), 1625-1628.

Jones, N. (2018). "How to stop data centres from gobbling up the world's electricity." Nature, 561, 163-166.

Strubell, E., et al. (2019). "Energy and Policy Considerations for Deep Learning in NLP." Proceedings of the 57th Annual Meeting of the Association for Computational Linguistics.

Rolnick, D., et al. (2022). "Tackling Climate Change with Machine Learning." ACM Computing Surveys, 55(2), 1-96.

TWENTY TWO

The New York Times' Copyright Lawsuit Against OpenAI Threatens the Future of AI and Fair Use

Aswin Prabhakar, Center for Data Innovation, January 2024

This report analyzes The New York Times' recent lawsuit against Microsoft and OpenAI over the use of its content in AI models. It argues that the lawsuit misrepresents how large language models (LLMs) function and could potentially hinder AI development. The article contends that training AI on publicly available internet content falls under fair use and draws parallels to historical technological disruptions in the media industry.

Key Findings

- **Lawsuit Claims:** NYT accuses AI services of unlawfully using its content. Demands dismantling of LLMs trained on its articles. Claims LLMs are "mass copying" machines that reproduce content verbatim.

- **AI Development and Fair Use:** Training LLMs on public internet content likely falls under fair use.

LLMs synthesize information rather than simply memorizing content. Transformative nature of AI use differs from original intent of news articles.

- **Historical Context:** Parallels drawn to past technological disruptions (e.g., printing press, radio, internet). Each advance initially challenged established media but led to richer ecosystems.

- **Legal and Ethical Considerations:** Copyright law focuses on context and purpose of alleged copying. Fair use principle applies to research and technological advancement. AI's diverse applications (e.g., medical diagnosis) demonstrate transformative use.

- **Market Competition:** AI systems do not directly compete as news sources. LLMs lack human reasoning and depth of analysis of traditional journalism. Copyright law does not protect facts and ideas.

Analysis

The article argues that The New York Times' lawsuit is more motivated by fear of technological disruption than by solid legal grounds. It contends that the newspaper's claims misrepresent how LLMs function, oversimplifying their complex mechanisms of information synthesis.

The author draws parallels to historical instances of technological disruption in media, suggesting that AI represents the latest iteration of this pattern. While acknowledging the challenges new technologies pose to established industries, the article emphasizes the potential for AI to lead to a more diverse and innovative information ecosystem.

The report highlights the importance of the fair use doctrine in copyright law, particularly in the context of research and technological advancement. It argues that training AI models on publicly available internet content should be considered fair use due to its transformative nature and broad applications beyond the original intent of news articles.

The article also challenges the notion that AI systems directly compete with traditional news sources, emphasizing the continued value of human judgment and credibility in journalism. It suggests that while AI may compete in some areas, such as historical research, it does not threaten the core functions of current news reporting.

Recommendations

- **Legal Interpretation:** Courts should consider the transformative nature of AI training when applying the fair use doctrine.

- **Policy Development:** Policymakers should uphold the right of AI developers to train systems using publicly accessible internet data.

- **Technological Understanding:** Encourage better understanding of how LLMs actually function to inform legal and policy decisions.

- **Industry Adaptation:** Traditional media should focus on adapting to technological changes rather than resisting them through litigation.

- **Fair Use Guidelines:** Develop clearer guidelines for applying fair use principles to AI training and development.

Conclusion

While The New York Times' lawsuit raises important questions about copyright in the AI era, the article argues that it mischaracterizes the nature of AI development and could potentially hinder technological progress. As courts and policymakers grapple with these issues, it will be crucial to balance copyright protections with the transformative potential of AI technologies. The historical pattern of media adaptation to new technologies suggests that embracing rather than resisting AI could lead to a more diverse and innovative information landscape.

Further Reading

Samuelson, P. "AI Authorship?" Communications of the ACM, 2020.

Lemley, M.A. & Casey, B. "Fair Learning." Texas Law Review, 2020.

Grimmelmann, J. "Copyright for Literate Robots." Iowa Law Review, 2016.

Levendowski, A. "How Copyright Law Can Fix Artificial Intelligence's Implicit Bias Problem." Washington Law Review, 2018.

Sobel, B. "Artificial Intelligence's Fair Use Crisis." Columbia Journal of Law & the Arts, 2017.

TWENTY THREE

The Longtermist Fear of a Future Malevolent Superintelligence is Hindering our Progress Today

Paula Gürtler, Centre for European Policy Studies, January 2024

This article critiques the philosophy of longtermism and its influence on AI regulation. It argues that while long-term thinking is important, the longtermist approach to AI policy needs to be revised and could mislead policymakers. The author contends that the EU's AI Act, which focuses on concrete, near-term regulations, offers a better model for global AI governance.

Key Findings

- **Rise of Longtermism in AI Discourse:** Increasing focus on existential risks from superintelligent AI. Influence on high-level discussions, including EU leadership and UK AI Safety Summit.

- **Longtermist Philosophy:** Prioritizes influencing long-term future over present concerns. Argues for zero discount rate in policymaking. Focuses on preventing worst-case scenarios like human extinction.

- **Flaws in Longtermist Approach:** Overlooks other existential threats (e.g., climate change, pandemics). Ignores AI's potential to mitigate other risks. Fails to weigh competing goals beyond human survival.

- **Impact on AI Policymaking:** Distracts from regulating current AI systems affecting everyday life. Overlooks near-term benefits and risks of AI technology. May hinder AI development that could address pressing issues.

- **EU AI Act as Alternative Model:** Focuses on concrete, applicable rules for current AI systems. Balances innovation with risk mitigation. Could inspire more pragmatic approach to global AI governance.

Analysis

The article argues that the longtermist approach to AI policy needs to be revised in its methodology and priorities. By focusing exclusively on preventing hypothetical far-future catastrophes, longtermists overlook more immediate and tangible risks and the potential benefits of AI development.

The author contends that good policymaking requires weighing multiple factors and considering both short-term and long-term impacts. The longtermist approach, with its zero discount rate and single-minded focus on human extinction, needs to account for the complexity of policy decisions and the multiple goals societies may have beyond mere survival.

The article suggests that the EU's AI Act, which focuses on regulating current AI systems and balancing innovation with risk mitigation, offers a better model for AI governance. This approach allows for addressing immediate concerns while still considering long-term impacts, without being paralyzed by speculative far-future scenarios.

Recommendations

- **Balanced Approach:** Policymakers should consider both short-term and long-term impacts of AI, without overly prioritizing speculative far-future risks.

- **Comprehensive Risk Assessment:** Include a wider range of existential threats in AI policy considerations, not just superintelligence.

- **Consider AI Benefits:** Recognize AI's potential to mitigate other risks and contribute to societal goals.

- **Pragmatic Regulation:** Focus on concrete, applicable rules for current AI systems, as exemplified by the EU AI Act.

- **Multi-faceted Goals:** Consider a range of societal objectives beyond mere survival when crafting AI policy.

- **Improved Methodology:** Develop more robust methods for weighing competing policy goals across different time horizons.

Conclusion

While long-term thinking is valuable in policymaking, the longtermist approach to AI regulation must be revised and potentially counterproductive. Focusing exclusively on preventing hypothetical far-future catastrophes risks overlooking more immediate concerns and hindering beneficial AI development. The EU's AI Act, focusing on concrete, near-term regulations, offers a more balanced and pragmatic model for global AI governance. As other jurisdictions develop their AI policies, they should be wary of the limitations of longtermist thinking and strive for a more comprehensive approach that considers both present and future impacts.

Further Reading

Ord, T. "The Precipice: Existential Risk and the Future of Humanity." Hachette Books, 2020.

MacAskill, W. "What We Owe the Future." Basic Books, 2022.

Bostrom, N. "Superintelligence: Paths, Dangers, Strategies." Oxford University Press, 2014.

Gabriel, I. "Artificial Intelligence, Values, and Alignment." Minds and Machines, 2020.

European Commission. "Proposal for a Regulation on Artificial Intelligence." 2021.

TWENTY FOUR

Envisioning Africa's AI Governance Landscape in 2024

Melody Musoni, European Centre for Development Policy Management, January 2024

This policy brief explores anticipated developments shaping AI governance in Africa in 2024, focusing on the potential adoption of an African continental AI strategy and increased African participation in global AI governance. It emphasizes the need for African voices to have a meaningful impact in ensuring AI promotes socio-economic development in Africa.

Key Findings

- **Continental AI Strategy:** African Union (AU) expected to endorse a Continental Strategy on AI in February 2024. Strategy likely to articulate Africa's vision for AI governance and address challenges like limited use of African datasets.

- **National AI Strategies:** Increase expected in number of African countries developing national AI strategies. South Africa, Namibia, Côte D'Ivoire,

Nigeria, Kenya, and Ethiopia identified as likely leaders.

- **Data Protection Laws:** Push to support remaining 15 African countries without data protection laws to adopt them. Need to strengthen institutional capacities of data regulators to hold AI actors accountable.

- **Influence of EU AI Act:** European regulations likely to shape African AI governance through "Brussels Effect." African governments may borrow elements from EU AI Act for their own legislation.

- **Global AI Governance Participation:** Increased African representation expected in international AI forums. Opportunity for Africa to contribute to global AI policy discussions through AU's G20 membership.

- **African AI Innovation:** Governments encouraging investment in AI research and innovation. International partnerships and private sector investment crucial for growth.

- **AI Education and Awareness:** Surge expected in digital skills and AI literacy initiatives. Need for integration of AI education into broader digital skills programs.

Analysis

The brief highlights the critical importance of 2024 for shaping Africa's AI governance landscape. It emphasizes the need for a comprehensive, coordinated approach that integrates AI policy with broader digital governance initiatives. The author stresses the importance of African voices and perspectives in global AI discussions, moving beyond tokenism to ensure meaningful impact.

The potential adoption of a continental AI strategy by the AU is seen as a major milestone, potentially providing a blueprint for national strategies and articulating an "African approach" to AI governance. The brief notes the importance of addressing challenges like limited use of African datasets and algorithmic biases.

The influence of international regulations, particularly the EU AI Act, is expected to be significant. However, the author cautions against simply copying European approaches, emphasizing the need for African-specific solutions.

The brief also highlights the importance of building Africa's AI innovation ecosystem, noting that while some governments provide incentives, significant international and private sector investment will be crucial.

Recommendations

- Develop and implement a comprehensive AU AI Strategy that addresses African-specific challenges and values.

- Support remaining African countries in adopting data protection laws and strengthening regulatory capacities.

- Ensure meaningful African participation in global AI governance forums, moving beyond tokenism.

- Integrate AI governance into broader digital policy initiatives, including data protection, cybersecurity, and digital trade.

- Invest in AI education and awareness programs, targeting diverse societal groups.

- Create conducive environments for AI research and innovation to attract investment and nurture African AI startups.

- Leverage international partnerships to support infrastructure development and AI innovation.

Conclusion

2024 represents a critical year for shaping Africa's AI governance landscape. While challenges remain, there are significant opportunities for African countries to develop AI policies that promote socio-economic development while addressing unique regional concerns. Success will require coordination across governments, engagement with diverse stakeholders, and meaningful participation in global AI governance discussions.

Further Reading

African Union. "Digital Transformation Strategy for Africa (2020-2030)."

Gwagwa, A. et al. "Artificial Intelligence (AI) Deployments in Africa: Benefits, Challenges and Policy Dimensions." The African Journal of Information and Communication, 2020.

Rutenberg, I. et al. "Artificial Intelligence Governance in the African Context." Centre for Intellectual Property and Information Technology Law, Strathmore University, 2022.

UN Economic Commission for Africa. "Harnessing Emerging Technologies: The Cases of Artificial Intelligence and Nanotechnology." 2021.

World Bank. "The State of Digital Development in Africa." 2023.

TWENTY FIVE

Nuclear Arms Control Policies and Safety in Artificial Intelligence: transferable lessons or false equivalence?

Eoin Micheál McNamara, Finnish Institute of International Affairs, January 2024

Artificial intelligence (AI) is rapidly advancing, promising immense benefits for social development while also posing significant risks to human society. Without strong safeguards, AI could lead to widespread disinformation, social polarization, mass unemployment, and, in the most extreme scenarios, pose existential threats to humanity. These developments echo the emergence of nuclear weapons in the 1940s, which dramatically reshaped international politics and introduced new dangers to human existence.

As with AI today, nuclear weapons emerged swiftly, heralding unprecedented dangers for human existence. Analogies from nuclear arms control have been scrutinized for their potential to guide policies responding to great power competition in AI. While some see these analogies as constructive for understanding new AI challenges, others view them as an irrelevant distraction from creating novel frameworks to regulate AI's unique and unprecedented developments.

This Briefing Paper argues that policy value in AI safety can be achieved by adopting a broader perspective incorporating concepts from nuclear arms control. Parallels with previous nuclear arms racing warn that unbridled strategic competition in AI will hasten the proliferation of unsafe technologies. Norm institutionalization stigmatizing "nuclear taboos" through treaties like the Non-Proliferation Treaty (NPT) prompts greater urgency for global frameworks to morally discourage dangerous AI developments. Just as strategic stability and reciprocity for risk reduction resulted in competing Cold War superpowers pragmatically agreeing to arms reductions, similar logic can also reduce unsafe elements in today's AI race.

Key Findings

- **AI and Nuclear Weapons Parallels:** Both emerged rapidly with potential existential risks to humanity. Intense great power competition in development. Need for global governance frameworks.

- **Debate on Analogies:** Some see arms control parallels as helpful for understanding AI challenges. Critics argue they distract from AI's unique aspects requiring new approaches.

- **AI Arms Race Dynamics:** US and China as frontrunners, with EU lagging but still competitive.

Russia further behind but redirecting resources to military AI. Great power rhetoric often equates AI advancement with arms racing.

- **Epistemic Communities:** Experts play crucial role in shaping norms and regulations. AI communities more aligned with commercial interests than nuclear scientists were.

- **Regulatory Approaches:** US balancing safety and innovation. EU developing comprehensive risk-based framework. China prioritizing algorithm safety and party interests.

- **Concepts for Further Exploration:** Strategic stability for mutual AI safety principles. Graduated Reciprocation in Tension Reduction (GRIT) for risk reduction initiatives. NPT-like global treaty to stigmatize dangerous AI developments.

Analysis

The paper argues that while there are clear differences between nuclear weapons and AI, some arms control concepts can provide valuable perspectives for AI governance. It emphasizes that the current framing of AI development as an arms race risks accelerating unsafe practices.

The author notes that unlike nuclear weapons, AI is being primarily driven by private industry rather than governments. This creates new challenges for regulation and safety oversight. The paper also highlights the differing regulatory approaches the US, EU, and China are taking, noting the uncertainty around which framework will have the most global influence.

The briefing suggests that concepts like strategic stability and GRIT could be adapted to promote mutual adoption of AI safety principles among great powers. It also proposes that an NPT-like global treaty could help stigmatize particularly dangerous AI developments, while acknowledging the greater complexity of AI compared to nuclear technology.

Recommendations

- Explore adapting arms control concepts like strategic stability and GRIT to AI governance.

- Consider developing a global multilateral treaty to stigmatize dangerous AI practices.

- Strengthen international dialogue on AI safety, particularly between the US, China, and EU.

- Recognize the limits of arms control analogies while leveraging relevant insights.

- Address the tension between market-driven AI innovation and government safety regulations.

- Support epistemic communities in AI to provide ethical and normative expertise for policymaking.

Conclusion

While arms control analogies have limitations when applied to AI, a broader examination of arms control geopolitics can provide both irrelevant and valuable parallels to assist in developing global security governance for AI. The paper emphasizes the need for multilateral management of AI development to avert irreversible societal problems, while recognizing the unique challenges posed by AI's widespread nature and rapid advancement.

Further Reading

Maas, M.M. "How Viable is International Arms Control for Military Artificial Intelligence? Three Lessons from Nuclear Weapons." Contemporary Security Policy, 2019.

Tannenwald, N. "Stigmatizing the Bomb: Origins of the Nuclear Taboo." International Security, 2005.

Baker, M. "Nuclear Arms Control Verification and Lessons for AI Treaties." Computers and Society, 2023.

Khlaaf, H. "How AI Can Be Regulated Like Nuclear Energy." Time, 2023.

Collins, A. "GRIT, Gorbachev and the End of the Cold War." Review of International Studies, 1998.

TWENTY SIX

Algorithms By and For the Workers

Bonn Juego, Tereza Østbø Kuldova and Gerard Rinse Oosterwijk, Foundation for European Progressive Studies, January 2024

This report analyzes a policy study by the Foundation for European Progressive Studies (FEPS) and Nordic partners on the impact of Algorithmic Management (AM) on workers' rights and well-being. The study examines the challenges posed by workplace digitalization, particularly the rise of AM, and argues for strengthening worker participation and co-determination in shaping digital transitions. It highlights the limitations of current policies and institutions in addressing these challenges and proposes a framework for more worker-centric approaches to AI governance.

The digitalization of workplaces, driven by competitive pressures in global capitalism, is rapidly transforming labor relations worldwide. A key manifestation of this transformation is the increasing use of algorithmic management (AM), which are computer-programmed systems that monitor, evaluate, and control workers' behavior and performance. This policy study reflects on the complex interplay between technology and work, focusing on the impacts of AM on workers' rights, dignity, and well-being.

Key Findings

- **Rise of Algorithmic Management:** AM is increasingly prevalent across various sectors, from digital platforms to traditional workplaces. Driven by capitalist imperatives for efficiency, optimization, and profit maximization. Promises increased productivity and data-driven decision-making. Raises concerns about labor exploitation, work intensification, and erosion of worker autonomy.

- **Challenges to Workers' Rights:** AM often lacks transparency, raising accountability issues. Risk of perpetuating or exacerbating biases and discrimination. Potential for increased surveillance and control of workers. Erosion of worker privacy and data protection rights. Undermining of professional judgment and discretion in some fields.

- **Policy and Institutional Limitations:** Current regulatory frameworks (e.g., GDPR, EU AI Act) insufficient to address AM-specific challenges. Fragmented global governance landscape for AI and digital technologies. Lack of worker-specific protections in many AI governance proposals. Gap between theoretical protections and practical implementation.

- **Worker Agency and Co-determination:** Nordic model of workplace democracy challenged by AM. Importance of collective bargaining and worker representation in AI governance. Potential for "digital co-determination" to empower workers in technology decisions. Need to strengthen institutions supporting worker participation.

- **Contextual Differences:** AM impacts vary across industries, countries, and regulatory environments. Importance of considering national institutions, legal frameworks, and labor organization. Need for context-specific research and policy approaches.

Analysis

The policy study argues that while AM and broader digitalization trends offer potential benefits, they also pose significant risks to workers' rights and well-being. The authors emphasize that current policy frameworks are struggling to keep pace with technological changes, leaving gaps in worker protections.

A key theme of the study is the importance of worker agency and participation in shaping digital transitions. The authors draw inspiration from the Nordic model of co-determination, which institutionalizes worker involvement in organizational decision-making. However, they note that even this model is under pressure from AM and other digital technologies that can bypass traditional consultation processes.

The study highlights the complexities and contradictions of AM implementation. While it can increase efficiency and provide data-driven insights, it also risks intensifying work, eroding worker autonomy, and perpetuating biases. The authors argue that these challenges require a multifaceted response involving policy, institutional reform, and worker empowerment.

A significant contribution of the study is its emphasis on context-specific approaches. The authors recognize that AM's impacts and potential solutions vary across different sectors, countries, and regulatory environments. This nuanced view challenges one-size-fits-all policy approaches and calls for more tailored research and interventions.

Recommendations

- Develop comprehensive AI governance frameworks that prioritize workers' rights and well-being

- Strengthen collective bargaining institutions to address AM challenges effectively

- Promote "digital co-determination" to give workers a voice in technology implementation decisions

- Conduct context-specific research to inform tailored policy solutions for different sectors and countries

- Invest in worker education and upskilling to navigate digital transitions

- Create public institutions to steer pro-worker digital transformations

- Explore the potential of AI to enhance rather than undermine worker empowerment

- Establish stronger mechanisms for algorithmic transparency and accountability

- Develop industry-specific guidelines for ethical AM implementation

- Foster international cooperation on AI governance while respecting national contexts

---

Conclusion

The policy study makes a compelling case for a more worker-centric approach to managing the digital transformation of work. It emphasizes the need for policies and institutions that can harness the benefits of AI and algorithmic systems while protecting workers' rights and promoting their active participation in shaping the future of work.

The authors' call for context-specific, problem-based, and mission-oriented research is particularly noteworthy. This approach recognizes the complexity of AM's impacts across diverse work settings and the need for nuanced policy responses. By advocating for a more participatory and inclusive approach to AI governance, the study contributes valuable insights to ongoing debates about the future of work in the digital age. To build on this study's findings, future research could focus on:

- Comparative analysis of AM implementation and impacts across different countries and sectors

- Evaluation of existing co-determination models in addressing AM challenges

- Development and testing of "digital co-determination" frameworks

- Assessment of the effectiveness of current AI governance initiatives in protecting workers' rights

- Exploration of potential synergies between worker empowerment and technological innovation

---

Further Reading

Aloisi, A. & De Stefano, V. (2022). Your Boss is an Algorithm. Oxford: Bloomsbury Publishing.

Kellogg, K., Valentine, M., & Christin, A. (2020). "Algorithms at Work: The New Contested Terrain of Control." Academy of Management Annals, 14(1): 366-410.

Moore, P., Upchurch, M., & Whittaker, X. (eds) (2018). Humans and Machines at Work: Monitoring, Surveillance and Automation in Contemporary Capitalism. Cham: Palgrave Macmillan.

Pasquale, F. (2015). The Black Box Society: The Secret Algorithms that Control Money and Information. Cambridge, MA: Harvard University Press.

Zuboff, S. (2019). The Age of Surveillance Capitalism: The Fight for a Human Future at the New Frontier of Power. London: PublicAffairs.

Twenty Seven

The Promise and Peril of AI in the Power Grid

Ismael Arciniegas Rueda, Henri van Soest, Hye Min Park, Rand Corporation, January 2024

This report explores the transformative potential and inherent risks of integrating artificial intelligence (AI) into the power grid. AI can revolutionize the energy sector by optimizing energy consumption, improving efficiency, forecasting energy demand and supply, and facilitating the integration of renewable energy sources. However, significant challenges, particularly the outdated infrastructure of current power grids, must be addressed to realize these benefits fully.

Key Findings

- **Optimization of Energy Consumption:** AI can significantly reduce waste and enhance efficiency in energy consumption.

- **Enhanced Forecasting:** AI's predictive capabilities can help prevent blackouts and improve grid flexibility.

- **Integration of Renewable Energy:** AI can better predict the availability of renewable energy sources, optimizing their integration into the grid.

- **Infrastructure Challenges:** The current outdated infrastructure poses a significant barrier to AI integration, necessitating substantial investment for modernization.

Analysis

The power sector is undergoing a significant transformation, driven by increasing demand for electricity and the imperative to decarbonize energy production. As the complexity of power grids escalates, the need for advanced analytical tools like AI becomes more pronounced. AI's ability to process and analyze vast amounts of data at high speeds and volumes positions it as a crucial technology for managing future power grids.

Optimization of Energy Consumption

AI can optimize energy consumption by analyzing usage patterns and making real-time adjustments to reduce waste and improve efficiency. For instance, AI algorithms can identify peak usage times and adjust energy distribution accordingly, ensuring energy is used more efficiently and reducing the overall consumption footprint. This optimization extends to various applications, from residential energy use to industrial processes, where AI can streamline operations and minimize energy wastage.

Enhanced Forecasting

One significant advantage of AI in the power grid is its ability to accurately forecast energy demand and supply. AI models can analyze historical data and predict future energy needs, allowing energy providers to adjust their production and distribution strategies. This predictive capability helps prevent blackouts and ensure a stable energy supply. For example, during peak demand periods, AI can predict the surge in energy use and preemptively adjust the grid to accommodate the increased load, thereby maintaining stability and preventing outages.

Integration of Renewable Energy

Renewable energy sources, such as solar and wind power, are inherently intermittent and unpredictable. AI can mitigate these challenges by better predicting when these energy sources will be available and adjusting energy storage and consumption accordingly. For instance, AI can forecast weather patterns to predict solar and wind energy production, allowing for more efficient integration of these sources into the grid. This capability is crucial for maximizing the use of renewable energy and reducing reliance on fossil fuels, thereby contributing to a more sustainable energy system.

Infrastructure Challenges

Despite the numerous benefits, integrating AI into the power grid is not without its challenges. The most significant barrier is the outdated infrastructure of many power grids, built decades ago and not equipped to handle the demands of modern technologies. These outdated systems need the necessary digital infrastructure to support AI applications, making it difficult to leverage AI's full potential. To address this, substantial investments are required to modernize the grid, including upgrading physical infrastructure and implementing advanced digital systems that can support AI integration.

Case Studies and Real-World Examples

Several real-world examples highlight the potential of AI in the power sector. For instance, in the United States, companies like Grid4C use AI to predict energy consumption patterns and optimize energy use in residential homes. By analyzing data from smart meters, Grid4C's AI algorithms can make real-time adjustments to energy consumption, reducing waste and improving efficiency.

In Europe, the TSO2020 project is leveraging AI to enhance grid stability and integrate renewable energy sources. The project uses AI to analyze data from various sources, including weather forecasts and energy consumption patterns, to predict energy production from renewable sources and adjust grid operations accordingly.

These examples demonstrate the practical applications of AI in the power sector and the tangible benefits it can deliver in terms of efficiency, reliability, and sustainability.

Recommendations

- **Upgrade Infrastructure:** Invest in modernizing the power grid infrastructure to support AI integration. This includes upgrading physical infrastructure and implementing advanced digital systems that can handle the data processing and analytical demands of AI.

- **Training and Development:** Implement training programs for operators to effectively manage AI tools and technologies. This will ensure that the workforce is equipped with the necessary skills to leverage AI effectively and maximize its potential.

- **Regulatory Support:** Advocate for policies that support infrastructure investment and AI implementation in the energy sector. Regulatory frameworks should encourage innovation and provide incentives for investments in modernizing the grid and adopting AI technologies.

- **Pilot Projects:** Initiate pilot projects to test AI applications in real-world grid scenarios. These projects can serve as test beds for evaluating the effectiveness and scalability of AI technologies, providing valuable insights that can inform broader deployment strategies.

Conclusion

Integrating AI in the power grid offers promising opportunities to enhance efficiency and reliability and integrate renewable energy sources. However, realizing these benefits requires addressing the significant challenge of outdated infrastructure through substantial investment and supportive policies. By modernizing the grid and leveraging AI's capabilities, the power sector can achieve a more sustainable and efficient energy system, better equipped to meet the demands of the future.

Further Reading

Ismael Arciniegas Rueda, Henri van Soest, Hye Min Park, "The Promise and Peril of AI in the Power Grid," RAND Corporation, 2024.

Pew Research Center, "Slightly fewer Americans are reading print books, new survey finds," 2023.

Comfy Living, "21 Captivating Reading Statistics and Facts for 2024."

Grid4C Case Study: Analyzing AI's impact on residential energy consumption and efficiency.

TSO2020 Project: Exploring AI's role in enhancing grid stability and integrating renewable energy in Europe.

TWENTY EIGHT

AI Poses Risks to Both Authoritarian and Democratic Politics

Alla Polishchuk, Wilson Center, January 2024

This report explores the expanding use of artificial intelligence (AI) in political contexts, focusing on both its potential benefits and the significant risks it poses to democratic and authoritarian regimes. AI's role in electoral processes has increased, as evidenced by recent elections in Argentina, Turkey, and Russia. The integration of AI in political strategies highlights its dual capacity to enhance political campaigns and undermine democratic institutions through disinformation and manipulation.

Key Findings

- **AI in Electoral Campaigns:** AI is being used to create persuasive content and deepfakes to influence voter behavior and outcomes.

- **Disinformation Risks:** The spread of AI-generated misinformation can erode trust in democratic institutions.

- **Authoritarian Uses of AI:** Authoritarian regimes are using AI to suppress dissent and manipulate public opinion.

- **Regulatory Challenges:** Current regulatory frameworks are inadequate to address the rapid advancements and misuse of AI in politics.

Analysis

AI in Electoral Campaigns

AI has become a powerful tool in political campaigns, as seen in the 2023 presidential elections in Argentina and Turkey. In Argentina, AI was used to generate videos that both promoted candidates and attacked opponents. For instance, Sergio Massa's campaign created a deepfake video of his rival, Javier Milei, discussing the hypothetical sale of human organs, which, despite being labeled as AI-generated, spread widely without disclaimers. This tactic exemplifies the potential of AI to shape political narratives and influence voter perceptions.

In Turkey, President Recep Tayyip Erdoğan's campaign utilized AI-generated videos to falsely depict his main opponent, Kemal Kiliçdaroğlu, as being endorsed by a terrorist organization. This manipulation shaped public opinion and contributed to Erdoğan's victory, showcasing how AI can be weaponized in electoral politics to devastating effect.

Disinformation Risks

The proliferation of AI-generated disinformation poses a severe threat to democratic processes. AI can create realistic but false content, such as deepfake videos and misleading social media posts, which can misinform the public and undermine trust in democratic institutions. For example, during the Russian invasion of Ukraine, hackers uploaded a deepfake video of President Volodymyr Zelensky urging Ukrainian soldiers to surrender. Such tactics are designed to destabilize societies and erode trust in leadership and institutions.

Authoritarian Uses of AI

In authoritarian regimes, AI is increasingly used to maintain control and suppress dissent. Russia, for instance, employs AI to create deepfake content to discredit political opponents and anti-war activists. The Kremlin's use of AI to produce multiple conflicting narratives aims to confuse and manipulate public opinion, thereby maintaining its grip on power. This use of AI highlights its potential to support authoritarian practices by controlling information and stifling opposition.

Regulatory Challenges

Addressing the challenges posed by AI in politics requires robust regulatory frameworks. Current efforts by the European Parliament and the US Federal Election Commission to regulate AI in political messaging are steps in the right direction, but more comprehensive measures are needed. Enhancing privacy protections, improving transparency in AI-generated content, and holding tech companies accountable for the spread of disinformation are essential actions to mitigate the risks associated with AI in politics.

Recommendations

- **Enhance Regulatory Frameworks:** Develop comprehensive regulations to govern the use of AI in political campaigns and disinformation.

- **Promote Transparency:** Require clear labeling of AI-generated content to inform the public about the nature of the information they consume.

- **Strengthen Privacy Protections:** Implement measures to safeguard personal data and limit its use in targeted disinformation campaigns.

- **Invest in Public Awareness:** Educate the public about the risks of AI-generated disinformation and how to identify and report it.

- **Encourage Responsible AI Use:** Advocate for ethical guidelines and best practices for AI use in politics to ensure it supports democratic values.

Conclusion

AI's integration into politics presents both opportunities and significant risks. While AI can enhance campaign strategies and voter engagement, its potential to spread disinformation and support authoritarian practices poses a grave threat to democratic institutions. Addressing these challenges requires comprehensive regulatory frameworks, increased transparency, and public awareness initiatives to safeguard the integrity of political processes.

Further Reading

Alla Polishchuk, "AI Poses Risks to Both Authoritarian and Democratic Politics," Wilson Center, 2024.

RAND Corporation, "The Promise and Peril of AI in the Power Grid," 2024.

Pew Research Center, "Slightly fewer Americans are reading print books, new survey finds," 2023.

TechHQ, "What's behind X hiring content moderation staff and allowing political advertising again?" 2023.

TWENTY NINE

A Cluster Analysis of National AI Strategies

James S. Denford, Gregory S. Dawson, and Kevin C. Desouza,
Brookings Institution, December 2023

This report provides an in-depth analysis of national AI strategies across various countries, focusing on their approaches to AI governance, capability development, and industry deployment. By comparing these strategies, we uncover significant differences and similarities in how nations address the opportunities and challenges posed by AI. The findings highlight the varying degrees of focus on data management, algorithmic management, AI governance, and public service orientation, providing insights into the future directions of AI policy and implementation.

Key Findings

- **Diverse Approaches to AI Governance:** Countries exhibit significant differences in their AI governance strategies, with varying levels of emphasis on ethics, transparency, and trust.

- **Cluster Analysis of AI Strategies:** Nations are grouped into clusters based on their AI strategy attributes, revealing leaders and laggards in AI adoption and governance.

- **Focus on Capability Development:** Countries prioritize different aspects of AI capability development, from education and research to business model innovation.

- **Industry and Public Service Applications:** AI deployment varies across industries, with some countries focusing on sectors like healthcare and energy, while others lag in strategic focus.

Analysis

AI Governance

AI governance encompasses the policies and frameworks that ensure ethical AI development and deployment. The analysis categorizes countries into high, medium, and low clusters based on their focus on AI security, regulations, social inequality impacts, and intellectual property rights protection. The high cluster includes countries like the US, Germany, and unexpectedly, China and Russia, indicating a robust approach to AI governance. These countries emphasize comprehensive governance measures but may differ in implementation fidelity.

Algorithmic Management

Algorithmic management focuses on the ethical use of AI algorithms, addressing issues like bias, transparency, and trust. Countries such as the US and Australia lead in this area, emphasizing the importance of ethical AI practices. Surprisingly, Russia also falls into this high cluster, despite its authoritarian tendencies. The low cluster, including Canada and China, shows minimal focus on these ethical considerations, highlighting a potential risk area for AI misuse.

Data Management

Effective data management, involving data exchange regulations, privacy, and security, is crucial for AI development. High cluster countries like the US and India prioritize internal data management but are cautious about international data sharing. Medium cluster countries, including the UK and Belgium, show a balanced approach, emphasizing data exchange while maintaining privacy concerns. The low cluster, with countries like Austria and Canada, indicates a need for more mature data management strategies, possibly due to nascent AI development stages.

Capability Development

Capability development strategies vary significantly, with countries focusing on different sources for AI skill enhancement. The high cluster, including the US and India, leverages various sources from R&D to higher education. The medium cluster, with countries like China and Australia, emphasizes education over research, while the low cluster, including Canada and Russia, focuses primarily on basic education and R&D. These differences reflect the varied priorities and maturity levels in national AI strategies.

Industry and Public Service Orientation

AI deployment across industries and public services shows distinct patterns. High cluster countries, such as the US and China, plan to integrate AI into multiple sectors, including technology, healthcare, and energy. The medium cluster focuses on key industries like agriculture and healthcare, while the low cluster needs a strategic focus, indicating missed opportunities for AI applications. In public services, the high cluster addresses broad areas, including healthcare, transportation, and defense, reflecting an all-encompassing growth strategy. The medium cluster prioritizes infrastructure, whereas the low cluster focuses on limited areas like healthcare, indicating a social welfare orientation.

Recommendations

- **Strengthen AI Governance:** Countries should develop comprehensive AI governance frameworks that address ethical concerns, transparency, and trust to ensure responsible AI development.

- **Enhance Data Management:** Improve data management strategies to balance data privacy and security with data sharing and collaboration benefits.

- **Prioritize Capability Development:** Invest in diverse AI capability development sources, including education, research, and business innovation, to build a robust AI ecosystem.

- **Expand Industry Applications:** Encourage AI deployment across various industries to leverage its full potential and drive economic growth.

- **Focus on Public Services:** Integrate AI into public services to enhance efficiency and effectiveness, particularly in critical areas like healthcare and transportation.

Conclusion

The analysis of national AI strategies reveals significant variations in how countries approach AI governance, capability development, and industry deployment. While some nations lead with comprehensive strategies, others lag, indicating potential areas for improvement. Countries can better harness AI's potential while mitigating associated risks by adopting best practices and addressing identified gaps.

Further Reading

James S. Denford, Gregory S. Dawson, Kevin C. Desouza, "A Cluster Analysis of National AI Strategies," Brookings, 2023.

RAND Corporation, "The Promise and Peril of AI in the Power Grid," 2024.

Pew Research Center, "Slightly fewer Americans are reading print books, new survey finds," 2023.

Wilson Center, "AI Poses Risks to Both Authoritarian and Democratic Politics," 2024.

THIRTY

New Technologies in the Workplace: a round-up of project research

Laura Nurski, Bruegel, December 2023

This report examines the integration of new technologies, particularly artificial intelligence (AI), in the workplace and its impact on job quantity, quality, and nature, as well as worker wellbeing. The analysis focuses on the slow but steady adoption of AI in Europe and the barriers hindering its broader implementation. By synthesizing various research findings, this report aims to provide a comprehensive overview of how AI is reshaping the workforce and the necessary steps to maximize its benefits while mitigating potential downsides.

Key Findings

- **AI Adoption in Europe:** AI adoption in Europe lags behind the US and China due to barriers such as insufficient human capital, data availability, and funding.

- **Employment Effects of AI:** AI impacts jobs across the skills spectrum, with significant effects on middle-skilled and low-skilled employment.

- **Job Quality and AI:** The use of AI in task management and surveillance has mixed effects on job quality, often leading to increased efficiency at the expense of worker wellbeing.

- **Worker Involvement:** Successful AI integration in the workplace requires active participation from workers during the implementation phase.

Analysis

AI Adoption in Europe

The adoption of AI in European workplaces is progressing slowly due to several barriers. European firms need help in terms of human capital, data availability, and funding, which impede the widespread implementation of AI technologies. To accelerate AI adoption, policymakers need to address these barriers by enhancing the labor market, financial market, and regulatory frameworks, as well as improving the basic digitization of businesses and technological infrastructure.

Employment Effects of AI

AI's impact on employment varies across different skill levels. While previous technological advancements led to job polarization, affecting primarily middle-skilled jobs, AI has the potential to alter both middle-skilled and low-skilled employment significantly. High-skilled jobs are less at risk, but the transformation must be revised. Policymakers should focus on supporting the re- and upskilling of workers to mitigate the negative effects of job displacement and ensure a smooth transition to new jobs created by AI.

Job Quality and AI

AI's influence on job quality is multifaceted. Algorithmic management, which includes using AI for task assignment and worker surveillance, can improve efficiency but often at the cost of worker well-being. Implementing AI-driven surveillance and evaluation systems can increase stress and decrease job satisfaction among workers. Therefore, it's crucial to include job quality measures in health and safety risk assessments for AI systems in the workplace.

Worker Involvement

For AI to be successfully integrated into the workplace, involving workers in the development and implementation phases is essential. When workers perceive new technologies as valuable and easy to use, they are more likely to embrace them. Employers, AI developers, and regulators should work together to ensure that AI systems are transparent, fair, and customizable to meet the needs of end-users. This approach will help align technology use with job requirements and improve overall acceptance and effectiveness.

Recommendations

- **Enhance AI Governance:** Develop robust frameworks to ensure the ethical use of AI, focusing on transparency, fairness, and trust.

- **Improve Data Management:** Address data privacy, security, and availability issues to support AI adoption.

- **Support Skill Development:** Implement policies for re- and upskilling workers to prepare them for the changes brought by AI.

- **Foster Worker Participation:** Encourage workers' active involvement in AI implementation to ensure that technologies meet their needs and improve job satisfaction.

- **Promote Job Quality:** Include job quality measures in AI system evaluations to mitigate negative impacts on worker wellbeing.

Conclusion

The integration of AI in the workplace presents both opportunities and challenges. While AI can enhance efficiency and create new job roles, it also poses risks to job quality and employment stability. By addressing the barriers to AI adoption, supporting skill development, and involving workers in the implementation process, policymakers and businesses can maximize the benefits of AI while mitigating its potential downside.

Further Reading

Laura Nurski, "New technologies in the workplace: a round-up of project research," Bruegel, 2023.

RAND Corporation, "The Promise and Peril of AI in the Power Grid," 2024.

Pew Research Center, "Slightly fewer Americans are reading print books, new survey finds," 2023.

Wilson Center, "AI Poses Risks to Both Authoritarian and Democratic Politics," 2024.

THIRTY ONE

Skills or a Degree: the rise of skills-based hiring for AI and green jobs

Eugenia Gonzalez Ehlinger and Fabian Stephany, Bruegel, December 2023

This report examines the shift from degree-based to skills-based hiring practices, particularly in artificial intelligence (AI) and green jobs. Using a dataset of around one million online job vacancies in the UK between 2019 and 2022, this analysis highlights how employers increasingly value specific skills over formal educational qualifications. The findings suggest that AI roles are particularly skills-intensive and offer significant wage premiums for specific skills. In contrast, green jobs still maintain some emphasis on formal education but also show a growing trend toward skills-based hiring.

Key Findings

- **Shift to Skills-Based Hiring:** Employers are placing more emphasis on individual skills rather than formal degrees, especially for AI and green jobs.

- **Wage Premiums for AI Skills:** AI roles offer significant wage premiums for specific skills, sometimes comparable to having a PhD.

- **Education Still Relevant for Green Jobs:** While skills are increasingly important, formal education still holds value for green jobs.

- **Broader Skill Sets Required:** AI and green jobs require a wider variety of skills compared to other job postings.

Analysis

Shift to Skills-Based Hiring

The analysis of job vacancies reveals a clear trend towards skills-based hiring in AI and green sectors. The demand for AI-related skills has more than doubled, while the requirement for university degrees in these roles has decreased by 23%. This shift indicates that employers are prioritizing practical skills that directly contribute to job performance over traditional educational credentials. For example, AI roles frequently require skills in machine learning, natural language processing, and neural networks, reflecting the specialized and technical nature of these positions.

Wage Premiums for AI Skills

AI roles demand a higher number of skills and offer substantial wage premiums for these skills. The regression analysis shows that AI skills can command a wage premium of 16%, similar to the premium for a PhD. This finding underscores the high value placed on technical expertise and practical skills in the AI field. Skills such as neural networks and natural language processing are particularly lucrative, reflecting their critical role in advanced AI applications.

Education Still Relevant for Green Jobs

While the trend towards skills-based hiring is evident, green jobs still significantly emphasize formal education. About 20% of green job postings require at least a university degree, and this requirement has remained stable over time. However, green jobs also demand broad skills, including environmental regulation, energy management, and waste management. This combination of formal education and practical skills suggests that green jobs are evolving to balance traditional qualifications with the need for specialized expertise.

Broader Skill Sets Required

Both AI and green jobs require a wider variety of skills compared to other sectors. AI roles typically list around 15 skills per posting, while green jobs list about seven. In contrast, other job postings average only four skills. This indicates that emerging fields like AI and green technologies demand specific technical skills and a diverse skill set to adapt to rapidly changing job requirements. This broader skill set includes technical competencies and soft skills, highlighting these roles' complex and interdisciplinary nature.

Recommendations

- **Enhance AI Governance:** Develop robust frameworks to ensure the ethical use of AI, focusing on transparency, fairness, and trust.

- **Improve Data Management:** Address data privacy, security, and availability issues to support AI adoption.

- **Support Skill Development:** Implement policies for re- and upskilling workers to prepare them for the changes brought by AI.

- **Foster Worker Participation:** Encourage active involvement of workers in AI implementation to ensure that technologies meet their needs and improve job satisfaction.

- **Promote Job Quality:** Include job quality measures in AI system evaluations to mitigate negative impacts on worker wellbeing.

Conclusion

The shift towards skills-based hiring in AI and green jobs represents a significant change in the labor market. While formal education remains important, particularly in green jobs, the increasing emphasis on specific skills highlights the need for a more flexible and adaptive approach to workforce development. By focusing on skills, employers can better meet the demands of emerging technologies and ensure that their workforce is prepared for the future.

Further Reading

Eugenia Gonzalez Ehrlinger, Fabian Stephany, "Skills or a degree? The rise of skill-based hiring for AI and green jobs," Bruegel, 2023.

RAND Corporation, "The Promise and Peril of AI in the Power Grid," 2024.

Pew Research Center, "Slightly fewer Americans are reading print books, new survey finds," 2023.

Wilson Center, "AI Poses Risks to Both Authoritarian and Democratic Politics," 2024.

THIRTY TWO

The Competitive Relationship Between Cloud Computing and Generative AI

Christophe Caraguati, Bruegel, December 2023

This report examines the competitive relationship between cloud computing and generative artificial intelligence (GenAI), focusing on their interdependence and the competition risks involved. Cloud providers offer essential infrastructure and services that GenAI providers need to train, run, and deploy their applications. Conversely, GenAI providers drive market growth for cloud services. However, this relationship also poses significant competition risks, including market concentration and anticompetitive practices. This report outlines these risks and provides recommendations for addressing them through regulatory and policy measures.

Key Findings

- **Interdependence of Cloud and GenAI:** Cloud and GenAI providers have a symbiotic relationship, with cloud infrastructure crucial for GenAI operations.

- **Market Concentration:** The relationship between cloud and GenAI providers can lead to increased market concentration among a few dominant players, known as hyperscalers.

- **Anticompetitive Practices:** Potential anticompetitive practices include discrimination in the supply of IT equipment, obstacles to interoperability, and self-preferencing.

- **Regulatory Gaps:** Existing competition laws and regulations may need to fully address the unique challenges posed by the cloud/GenAI relationship.

Analysis

Interdependence of Cloud and GenAI

Cloud computing and GenAI are pivotal to the digital economy, with the cloud sector in Europe expected to grow from €84.76 billion in 2022 to €175.87 billion by 2024. GenAI, similarly, is projected to increase from $6.33 billion to $35.94 billion in the same period. Cloud providers offer infrastructure-as-a-service (IaaS), platform-as-a-service (PaaS), and software-as-a-service (SaaS), which are essential for GenAI applications. For example, Microsoft Azure supports OpenAI's models, and Google Cloud collaborates with Cohere. These partnerships illustrate the critical role of cloud services in enabling GenAI operations.

Market Concentration

The increasing integration of GenAI with cloud services is leading to market concentration, with a few hyperscalers like Amazon Web Services (AWS), Google Cloud, and Microsoft Azure dominating the market. These firms benefit from economies of scale and scope, allowing them to offer comprehensive services and invest heavily in infrastructure and GenAI capabilities. However, this concentration can stifle competition, making it difficult for smaller providers to compete and for new entrants to penetrate the market.

Anticompetitive Practices

Several anticompetitive practices arise from the cloud/GenAI relationship:

- **Discrimination in IT Equipment Supply:** Dominant IT providers, such as Nvidia, may allocate critical resources like GPUs preferentially to larger cloud providers, disadvantaging smaller providers.

- **Interoperability Obstacles:** Cloud providers might limit the interoperability of GenAI solutions, creating barriers to switching and multi-cloud strategies.

- **Self-Preferencing:** Cloud providers may prioritize their GenAI tools and models over third-party solutions, reducing competition.

- **Tying and Bundling:** Practices like tying non-dominant services to dominant ones and bundling

GenAI solutions with cloud services can further entrench the market power of hyperscalers.

Regulatory Gaps

Current regulations, including merger control laws and antitrust rules, may need to adequately address the competition risks posed by cloud/GenAI partnerships. For instance, the European Merger Regulation (EUMR) focuses on changes in control, potentially overlooking partnerships that do not involve control but still have significant competitive influence. The Digital Markets Act (DMA) and the Data Act introduce some measures, such as interoperability requirements, but these need to be clarified and expanded to cover the full scope of potential issues.

Recommendations

- **Amend Regulatory Frameworks:** Update the EUMR to include partnerships with material competitive influence and specify interoperability requirements under the Data Act.

- **Enhance Monitoring:** Conduct regular market studies and involve international counterparts to monitor developments in the cloud and GenAI sectors.

- **Intervene Early:** Use fast procedural tools like interim measures to address imminent competition risks promptly.

- **Promote Open Standards:** Encourage the development of open standards for GenAI interoperability to foster competition and innovation.

- **Increase Transparency:** Require cloud and GenAI providers to disclose key terms of their partnerships and data usage practices to regulators.

Conclusion

The competitive relationship between cloud computing and GenAI is essential for the digital economy's growth but also poses significant competition risks. Addressing these risks requires updating regulatory frameworks, enhancing monitoring and enforcement, and promoting open standards and transparency. By taking these steps, policymakers can ensure that the benefits of cloud and GenAI technologies are realized without compromising competition and innovation.

Further Reading

Christophe Carugati, "The competitive relationship between cloud computing and generative AI," Bruegel, 2023.

RAND Corporation, "The Promise and Peril of AI in the Power Grid," 2024.

Pew Research Center, "Slightly fewer Americans are reading print books, new survey finds," 2023.

Wilson Center, "AI Poses Risks to Both Authoritarian and Democratic Politics," 2024.

Artificial Intelligence and Energy Consumption

Maria Demertzis, Bruegel, December 2023

This report delves into the interplay between artificial intelligence (AI) and energy consumption, highlighting the rapid growth of AI applications and the corresponding rise in energy demands. The analysis focuses on the implications of AI's energy consumption for sustainability and its challenges to achieving green energy goals. Drawing from recent studies and industry insights, this report outlines the current state of AI energy use, potential mitigation strategies, and the broader impact on global energy systems.

Key Findings

- **Significant Energy Consumption by AI:** AI applications, particularly large language models like ChatGPT, contribute significantly to global energy use.

- **Growth of AI Usage:** The number of AI users and applications is increasing rapidly, further driving up energy consumption.

- **Energy Efficiency Innovations:** Technological advancements are being developed to enhance energy efficiency in AI, but their impact is still being determined.

- **Ethical and Environmental Concerns:** AI's high energy consumption raises ethical and environmental issues, particularly in the context of global energy crises and sustainability goals.

Analysis

Significant Energy Consumption by AI

AI models require substantial computational power for training and operation, translating into significant energy use. For instance, an academic study estimates that by 2027, AI servers could consume as much electricity as Argentina does annually, accounting for about 0.5% of the world's total electricity consumption. This comparison underscores the scale of AI's energy demands and the need for effective energy management strategies.

Growth of AI Usage

The rapid adoption of AI technologies is a major driver of increased energy consumption. When OpenAI introduced ChatGPT, it reached 100 million users within two months, and by December 2023, it had over 180 million users. The proliferation of AI applications across various sectors, from entertainment to business, compounds this issue. Each application requires extensive data processing and storage capabilities, further increasing the energy load on data centers.

Energy Efficiency Innovations

While AI's energy consumption is a growing concern, there are ongoing efforts to improve energy efficiency in AI operations. Technological innovations aim to reduce the energy required for AI training and inference. For example, advancements in hardware, such as more efficient GPUs and specialized AI chips, are critical in this effort. However, it remains challenging to balance the rapid growth of AI with the pace of energy efficiency improvements.

Ethical and Environmental Concerns

The ethical implications of AI's energy consumption are significant, particularly in light of global energy challenges. During periods of high electricity prices, some countries have struggled to afford energy, leading to outages, while privileged regions continued to develop and use energy-intensive AI applications. This disparity raises questions about the equitable distribution of both the costs and benefits of AI innovations. Moreover, the reliance on fossil fuels for electricity generation exacerbates environmental concerns, as increased energy use contributes to higher carbon emissions.

Recommendations

- **Enhance AI Governance:** Develop comprehensive policies that address AI's energy consumption, focusing on sustainable practices and energy efficiency standards.

- **Promote Energy-Efficient AI Technologies:** Invest in research and development of more energy-efficient AI hardware and software solutions.

- **Encourage Sustainable Data Center Practices:** Implement regulations that promote using renewable energy sources in data centers and encourage energy-saving measures.

- **Increase Transparency and Accountability:** Require AI developers and operators to report on their energy usage and carbon footprint, promoting transparency and accountability.

- **Support Global Energy Equity:** Develop frameworks to ensure that the benefits of AI are distributed equitably, and the energy costs do not disproportionately impact disadvantaged regions.

Conclusion

AI's integration into various sectors offers immense potential but also poses significant energy challenges. The growing energy demands of AI applications highlight the need for sustainable practices and innovative solutions to mitigate their environmental impact. By enhancing governance, promoting energy-efficient technologies, and supporting equitable energy use, policymakers and industry leaders can balance the benefits of AI with the imperative of sustainability.

Further Reading

Maria Demertzis, "Artificial intelligence and energy consumption," Bruegel, 2023.

RAND Corporation, "The Promise and Peril of AI in the Power Grid," 2024.

Pew Research Center, "Slightly fewer Americans are reading print books, new survey finds," 2023.

Wilson Center, "AI Poses Risks to Both Authoritarian and Democratic Politics," 2024.

THIRTY FOUR

Policymakers Should use the SETI Model to Prepare for AI Doomsday Scenarios

Daniel Castro, Center for Data Innovation, December 2023

This report investigates the potential use of the SETI (Search for Extra-Terrestrial Intelligence) model to prepare for hypothetical AI doomsday scenarios. The SETI model, which involves monitoring and searching for extraterrestrial life, offers a structured approach to managing the existential risks posed by the development of Artificial General Intelligence (AGI). This report evaluates the merits and challenges of adopting a similar model for AI, emphasizing the need for international cooperation, rigorous scientific methods, and proactive policy-making to address the uncertainties and potential risks associated with AGI.

Key Findings

- **SETI Model Applicability:** The SETI model provides a useful framework for the systematic

192 • AI DIGEST VOL 2

search and monitoring of AGI, emphasizing international cooperation and scientific rigor.

- **Challenges of AGI Prediction:** There needs to be more skepticism and debate within the AI community regarding the feasibility and timeline of achieving AGI, complicating policy-making efforts.

- **Importance of Proactive Measures:** Early and proactive measures, including establishing a Search for Artificial General Intelligence (SAGI) Institute, are crucial to mitigate potential risks.

- **Ethical and Social Implications:** AGI's development and potential impact raise profound ethical and social questions that require careful consideration and inclusive dialogue.

Analysis

SETI Model Applicability

The SETI model's structured approach to searching for extraterrestrial intelligence can be adapted to monitor and manage AGI development. The SETI Institute's efforts since the 1980s, including global cooperation and rigorous scientific methods, provide a blueprint for addressing the uncertainties surrounding AGI. Establishing a SAGI Institute would involve similar principles: developing consensus on AGI indicators, designing experiments to detect AGI, and fostering international collaboration to share findings and manage risks.

Challenges of AGI Prediction

Predicting the development of AGI is fraught with challenges due to the need for more consensus among AI experts and the speculative nature of current AGI research. While some experts, like those at OpenAI, believe AGI could emerge within the next few decades, others remain skeptical, citing the numerous technical and philosophical hurdles that must be overcome. This uncertainty complicates efforts to develop robust policies and regulations, as the potential risks and timelines are not well-defined.

Importance of Proactive Measures

Proactive measures are essential to prepare for the potential advent of AGI. Establishing a SAGI Institute would centralize efforts to monitor AGI development and coordinate global responses. This institute could develop standardized tests to identify AGI, create protocols for post-detection actions, and serve as a clearinghouse for AGI-related research. Such an approach would help mitigate the risks of AGI while ensuring that beneficial AI innovations continue to advance.

Ethical and Social Implications

The development of AGI poses significant ethical and social challenges. Issues such as the potential for AGI to exacerbate economic inequalities, perpetuate biases, and disrupt social norms must be addressed through inclusive dialogue and ethical guidelines. Policymakers and researchers must consider the broader societal impacts of

AGI and ensure that its development aligns with human values and promotes global well-being.

Recommendations

- **Establish a SAGI Institute:** Create a dedicated institute to monitor and manage AGI development, modeled after the SETI Institute.

- **Promote International Cooperation:** Foster global collaboration to share research findings, develop consensus on AGI indicators, and coordinate responses to potential risks.

- **Develop Standardized Tests and Protocols:** Design standardized tests to identify AGI and establish protocols for post-detection actions to ensure a coordinated and effective response.

- **Encourage Ethical AI Development:** Develop and enforce ethical guidelines to address the social and ethical implications of AGI, ensuring that its development aligns with human values.

- **Increase Public Awareness and Dialogue:** Engage the public in discussions about AGI, its potential impacts, and the measures being taken to manage its risks, promoting transparency and inclusivity.

Conclusion

The SETI model offers a promising framework for addressing AGI's uncertainties and potential risks. By establishing a SAGI Institute, fostering international cooperation, and developing proactive measures, policymakers and researchers can better prepare for the advent of AGI while ensuring that its development benefits humanity. Addressing the ethical and social implications of AGI is crucial to promoting global well-being and maintaining public trust in AI technologies.

Further Reading

Daniel Castro, "Policymakers Should Use the SETI Model to Prepare for AI Doomsday Scenarios," Center for Data Innovation, 2023.

Reece Rogers, "What's AGI, and Why Are AI Experts Skeptical?" WIRED, 2023.

Maria Demertzis, "Artificial intelligence and energy consumption," Bruegel, 2023.

RAND Corporation, "The Promise and Peril of AI in the Power Grid," 2024.

Wilson Center, "AI Poses Risks to Both Authoritarian and Democratic Politics," 2024.

THIRTY FIVE

Artificial Intelligence and the Clustering of Human Capital: the risks for Europe

Bjöörn Brey and Erik van der Marel, European Centre for International Political Economy, December 2023

This report explores the impact of artificial intelligence (AI) on the clustering of human capital in Europe, assessing the risks and opportunities it presents. The study highlights how AI adoption is influenced by the availability and distribution of skilled human capital, particularly in science, technology, engineering, and mathematics (STEM). The findings indicate that Europe's uneven distribution of human capital could hinder its ability to fully leverage AI for economic growth, thereby exacerbating regional disparities and impacting long-term productivity.

Key Findings

- **Europe's Lag in AI Productivity:** Europe is trailing behind global leaders in AI productivity, with significant regional disparities in AI adoption and human capital availability.

- **Importance of STEM Graduates:** High level of STEM graduates are crucial for AI-driven growth, yet Europe faces a net outflow of these skills.

- **Persistent Regional Disparities:** Regions with historical investments in human capital show higher AI adoption rates, reinforcing long-term economic inequalities.

- **Policy Imperatives:** Effective policies are needed to attract and retain AI-related human capital and ensure Europe's global competitiveness.

Analysis

Europe's Lag in AI Productivity

Despite its potential, Europe must catch up with the leading regions in AI productivity. The continent's sluggish growth in productivity is partly due to its lag in adopting AI technologies compared to the US and China. The adoption of AI is critical for boosting productivity, but Europe's current trajectory suggests it may continue to fall behind unless significant changes are made.

Importance of STEM Graduates

A robust supply of STEM graduates is essential for AI to drive economic growth effectively. These graduates provide the technical skills needed to develop and implement AI technologies. However, Europe is experiencing a net outflow of STEM talent, which hampers its ability to compete in the AI domain. This brain drain is a significant obstacle to fostering a thriving AI ecosystem within Europe.

Persistent Regional Disparities

The distribution of human capital within Europe is highly uneven, with some regions significantly ahead in terms of AI adoption due to their historical investments in human capital. Regions that have consistently invested in education and skills development are now reaping the benefits through higher AI adoption rates. This trend indicates that without strategic interventions, regional disparities in AI adoption and economic growth will likely persist and possibly widen.

Policy Imperatives

To address these challenges, European policymakers must focus on creating an environment that attracts and retains AI talent. This includes investing in education, providing incentives for STEM graduates to stay and work in Europe, and fostering a culture of innovation. Policies should also aim to ensure that the benefits of AI are distributed equitably across all regions, preventing further economic disparities.

Recommendations

- **Enhance AI Governance:** Develop comprehensive frameworks to ensure ethical AI development, focusing on transparency, fairness, and accountability.

- **Invest in Education:** Increase funding for STEM education and provide scholarships and incentives to retain graduates within Europe.

- **Foster Innovation Hubs:** Create and support innovation hubs that attract global AI talent and facilitate collaboration between academia and industry.

- **Promote Regional Development:** Implement policies that support AI adoption in lagging regions to reduce disparities and promote balanced economic growth.

- **Encourage Public-Private Partnerships:** Leverage public-private partnerships to drive AI research and development, ensuring that advancements are shared across sectors.

Conclusion

AI has the potential to enhance economic growth and productivity in Europe significantly, but its benefits will not be fully realized without addressing the disparities in human capital distribution. By focusing on policies that attract and retain skilled professionals, fostering innovation, and ensuring equitable regional development, Europe can position itself as a competitive player in the global AI landscape. Effective governance and strategic investments in human capital are crucial to overcoming the current challenges and achieving sustainable AI-driven growth.

Further Reading

Björn Brey, Erik van der Marel, "Artificial Intelligence and the Clustering of Human Capital: The Risks for Europe," ECIPE, 2023.

Daniel Castro, "Policymakers Should Use the SETI Model to Prepare for AI Doomsday Scenarios," Center for Data Innovation, 2023.

Noah Berman, "What Is Artificial Intelligence (AI)?" Council on Foreign Relations, 2024.

RAND Corporation, "The Promise and Peril of AI in the Power Grid," 2024.

Wilson Center, "AI Poses Risks to Both Authoritarian and Democratic Politics," 2024.

THIRTY SIX

Philosophical Debates about AI Risks are a Distraction

James V. Marrone and Marek N. Posard, Rand Corporation, December 2023

This report examines the influence of Effective Altruism (EA) on artificial intelligence (AI) development and governance, with a focus on recent events at OpenAI. The philosophical movement of EA, rooted in utilitarianism, has gained significant traction in Silicon Valley, shaping discussions around AI safety and ethics. However, recent controversies have highlighted the potential pitfalls of EA's influence on AI governance. This report analyzes the implications of EA's role in AI development, using the OpenAI leadership crisis as a case study, and provides recommendations for a more balanced approach to AI governance.

Key Findings

- The EA movement has significantly influenced AI governance discussions, particularly regarding long-term risks and safety concerns.

- Recent events at OpenAI demonstrate the potential for conflicts between EA-influenced governance and business-oriented leadership in AI companies.

- The focus on hypothetical long-term AI risks may distract from addressing more immediate and concrete challenges posed by current AI technologies.

- EA's influence in the tech industry has been associated with some high-profile ethical lapses, raising questions about its effectiveness as a guiding philosophy for AI governance.

- There is a growing need for a more balanced approach to AI governance that considers both short-term and long-term impacts, as well as practical business considerations.

Analysis

Effective Altruism's Influence on AI Governance

Effective Altruism has emerged as a significant force in shaping discussions around AI development and governance, particularly in Silicon Valley. The movement's focus on maximizing overall good and considering long-term consequences has resonated with many tech leaders and researchers. In the context of AI, this has translated into a strong emphasis on AI safety and the potential long-term risks associated with advanced AI systems.

The recent leadership crisis at OpenAI serves as a prime example of how EA principles can impact AI governance. The OpenAI board, comprised of current and former effective altruists, apparently clashed with CEO Sam Altman over concerns related to AI safety and the company's direction. This conflict highlights the tension between EA-influenced governance focused on long-term risks and more business-oriented leadership concerned with short-term progress and profitability.

Challenges of EA-Influenced AI Governance

While the emphasis on AI safety is crucial, there are concerns that the EA approach may need to be more focused on hypothetical long-term risks at the expense of addressing more immediate challenges. As noted in the RAND commentary, "Philosophical Debates About AI Risks Are a Distraction," there is a risk of solving "purely theoretical problems that may not even need solving" while neglecting real-world issues such as bias in AI systems, labor market disruptions, and the spread of misinformation.

Furthermore, the association of EA with high-profile ethical lapses, such as the case of Sam Bankman-Fried and FTX, has raised questions about the movement's effectiveness as a moral compass for the tech industry. These incidents highlight the potential for EA principles to be misused or misinterpreted, leading to unintended negative consequences.

Balancing Long-Term Concerns with Practical Considerations

The OpenAI case demonstrates the need for a more balanced approach to AI governance that considers both long-term safety concerns and practical business realities. While the EA-influenced board's focus on AI safety is commendable, the abrupt removal of key leadership figures risks destabilizing the company and potentially slowing down important AI research and development.

A more effective approach would involve integrating EA principles with other ethical frameworks and practical considerations. This could include:

- Emphasizing evidence-based decision-making in AI governance

- Balancing long-term risk assessment with short-term impact evaluation

- Incorporating diverse perspectives beyond EA in AI ethics discussions

- Ensuring transparency and accountability in AI development processes

---

Recommendations

- Develop a more diverse ethical framework for AI governance incorporating EA principles alongside other perspectives and practical considerations.

- Addressing current, well-documented risks associated with AI technologies, such as bias, privacy concerns, and labor market disruptions, should be a priority.

- Establish clear guidelines for balancing long-term AI safety concerns with short-term development goals in AI companies and research institutions.

- Promote greater transparency in AI governance decisions, particularly in organizations with significant influence over AI development.

- Encourage ongoing dialogue between EA proponents, AI researchers, business leaders, and policymakers to develop a more comprehensive approach to AI ethics and governance.

Conclusion

Effective Altruism has significantly shaped discussions around AI development and governance, particularly concerning long-term risks and safety. However, recent events, such as the leadership crisis at OpenAI, have highlighted the potential pitfalls of an overly EA-influenced approach to AI governance. Moving forward, developing a more balanced framework that integrates EA principles with other ethical considerations and practical realities is crucial. By addressing both immediate and long-term concerns, the AI industry can work towards responsible innovation that maximizes benefits while minimizing risks.

Further Reading

Toby Ord, "The Precipice: Existential Risk and the Future of Humanity," Bloomsbury Publishing, 2020.

Nick Bostrom, "Superintelligence: Paths, Dangers, Strategies," Oxford University Press, 2014.

Stuart Russell, "Human Compatible: Artificial Intelligence and the Problem of Control," Viking, 2019.

Cass R. Sunstein, "The Ethics of Influence: Government in the Age of Behavioral Science," Cambridge University Press, 2016.

Kate Crawford, "Atlas of AI: Power, Politics, and the Planetary Costs of Artificial Intelligence," Yale University Press, 2021.

THIRTY SEVEN

The EU AI Act is a Cautionary Tale in Open-Source AI Regulation

Aswin Prabhakar, Center for Data Innovation, December 2023

This report examines the challenges and implications of regulating open-source artificial intelligence (AI) models, with a focus on the European Union's proposed AI Act. As open-source AI models gain prominence and influence in the tech industry, policymakers face the complex task of ensuring accountability and safety without stifling innovation and transparency. This report analyzes the potential impacts of the EU AI Act on open-source AI development, highlights key concerns raised by industry experts, and provides recommendations for a more balanced regulatory approach that preserves the benefits of open-source AI while addressing legitimate safety and ethical concerns.

Key Findings

- The EU AI Act, as currently proposed, would impose stringent requirements on open-source AI models, potentially creating significant barriers to their development and distribution.

- Open-source AI models generally perform better than closed-source models in complying with transparency and disclosure requirements related to training data and compute usage.

- Regulating the deployment and use of AI applications, rather than the underlying open-source models themselves, may be a more effective approach to addressing safety concerns.

- The EU AI Act's one-size-fits-all regulatory approach fails to account for the unique nature and benefits of open-source AI development.

- Balancing innovation, transparency, and accountability in AI regulation requires a nuanced approach that distinguishes between open-source and closed-source models.

Analysis

The EU AI Act and Open-Source AI Models

The European Union's proposed AI Act aims to establish a comprehensive regulatory framework for artificial intelligence systems. However, the current draft of the Act would impose the same stringent requirements on open-source foundation models as it does on closed-source models. This approach has raised concerns among industry experts and open-source advocates.

One of the proposed regulations' most problematic aspects is the requirement that providers of foundation models ensure compliance with a wide range of obligations, regardless of whether the model is provided as an open-source or commercial product. These obligations include risk mitigation strategies, data governance measures, and a ten-year documentation requirement.

Meeting these requirements could prove impractical and burdensome for open-source AI projects, which often involve decentralized collaboration and voluntary contributions from researchers and developers worldwide. For example, the proposed requirement to maintain extensive documentation for ten years after a foundation model is deployed raises questions about who would be responsible for this task in the context of open-source projects.

Transparency and Compliance

Interestingly, recent research from Stanford University indicates that open-source foundation models generally perform better than closed-source models in complying with transparency and disclosure requirements related to training data and compute usage. This finding suggests that open-source AI development already aligns well with some of the key objectives of the EU AI Act, particularly in terms of transparency and accountability.

The Stanford study found a clear dichotomy in compliance based on release strategy. Open-source models tended to score highly on resource disclosure requirements for both data and compute resources. In contrast, closed-source models performed better on deployment-related requirements, likely due to the greater control providers have over their use and distribution.

Challenges and Unintended Consequences

The one-size-fits-all approach of the EU AI Act could have several unintended consequences for the open-source AI ecosystem:

- **Innovation barriers:** Stringent compliance requirements could discourage researchers and developers from contributing to open-source AI projects, potentially slowing down innovation in the field.

- **Reduced transparency:** Regulations aimed at increasing transparency might push some AI development behind closed doors to avoid compliance burdens.

- **Competitive disadvantage:** Open-source AI projects, often operating with limited resources, may need help to meet the same regulatory requirements as well-funded commercial entities.

- **Global impact:** The EU AI Act could set a precedent for AI regulation worldwide, potentially influencing policies in other regions and affecting the global open-source AI ecosystem.

Recommendations

- Adopt a differentiated regulatory approach that recognizes open-source AI models' unique characteristics and benefits, distinguishing them from closed-source commercial systems.

- Focus regulation on deploying and using AI applications rather than the underlying open-source models themselves. This approach would address safety concerns while preserving the benefits of open-source development.

- Encourage the development of industry standards and best practices for open-source AI development that promote transparency, safety, and ethical considerations without imposing overly burdensome regulatory requirements.

- Establish clear guidelines for using copyrighted data in AI training, addressing one of the key areas where both open-source and closed-source models currently need to catch up in compliance.

- Promote international cooperation and dialogue to develop harmonized approaches to AI regulation that balance innovation, transparency, and accountability across different jurisdictions.

Conclusion

The regulation of open-source AI models presents a complex challenge for policymakers seeking to ensure safety and accountability in AI development while preserving the benefits of open innovation. The EU AI Act, while well-intentioned, risks creating significant barriers for open-source AI projects if implemented in its current form. A more nuanced approach that recognizes the unique nature of open-source development and focuses on regulating AI applications rather than foundation models could better achieve the goals of responsible AI development. By fostering collaboration between policymakers, industry experts, and the open-source community, it is possible to create a regulatory framework that promotes innovation, transparency, and accountability in the rapidly evolving field of artificial intelligence.

Further Reading

Bommasani, R., et al. "Do Foundation Model Providers Comply with the EU AI Act?," Stanford Center for Research on Foundation Models, 2023.

Prabhakar, A. "The EU AI Act Is a Cautionary Tale in Open-Source AI Regulation," Center for Data Innovation, 2023.

Craglia, M., et al. "Artificial Intelligence: A European Perspective," European Commission Joint Research Centre, 2022.

Brundage, M., et al. "Toward Trustworthy AI Development: Mechanisms for Supporting Verifiable Claims," arXiv preprint, 2020.

Cihon, P., et al. "Standards for AI Governance: International Standards to Enable Global Coordination in AI Research & Development," Future of Humanity Institute, University of Oxford, 2021.

THIRTY EIGHT

Generative AI: global governance and the risk-based approach

Gianclaudio Malgieri and Gautam Kamath, Centre on Regulation in Europe, November 2023

This report examines the emerging global governance frameworks for generative artificial intelligence (AI), focusing on the risk-based regulatory approach being developed in jurisdictions like the European Union. As generative AI technologies rapidly advance and spread, policymakers worldwide grapple with harnessing their benefits while mitigating potential risks. This report analyzes key challenges, policy developments, and recommendations for a balanced, internationally-coordinated approach to generative AI governance. The risk-based framework emerging from initiatives like the EU AI Act and the G7 Hiroshima AI Process offers a promising model for effective regulation that supports innovation while addressing safety and ethical concerns.

Key Findings

- Generative AI poses a complex set of potential risks, including the spread of misinformation, privacy and cybersecurity threats, environmental impacts, and labor market disruption.

- The EU's proposed AI Act introduces a risk-based regulatory framework that could serve as a model for other jurisdictions, classifying AI applications into risk tiers with corresponding obligations.

- Global policy initiatives like the G7 Hiroshima AI Process are working to establish common principles and standards for responsible AI development and use.

- There is growing consensus on the need for ex-ante risk assessment and mitigation measures for high-risk AI applications, including some foundation models.

- Multistakeholder governance approaches involving industry, civil society, and government will be crucial for developing effective and flexible regulatory frameworks.

Analysis

Risks and Challenges of Generative AI

Generative AI technologies like large language models have demonstrated remarkable capabilities but also raise significant concerns. Key risks identified include:

- Spread of misinformation and deepfakes, potentially impacting democratic processes

- Privacy violations and cybersecurity vulnerabilities

- Environmental impacts from high energy consumption

- Labor market disruption and potential job losses

- Bias and discrimination in AI outputs

- Concentration of power among a few AI companies

Policymakers face the challenge of addressing these risks while fostering innovation and realizing generative AI's potential benefits across sectors like healthcare, education, and scientific research.

Emerging Regulatory Approaches

The EU's proposed AI Act represents the most advanced regulatory framework for AI globally. Its risk-based approach classifies AI applications into different risk levels:

- **Unacceptable risk:** Prohibited applications that violate fundamental rights

- **High risk:** Applications in sensitive domains requiring ex-ante conformity assessments

- **Limited risk:** Applications with transparency requirements

- **Low/minimal risk:** Minimal to no obligations

This tiered system aims to impose proportionate obligations based on an AI system's potential for harm. The

EU is also considering specific requirements for general-purpose AI models that could be used in high-risk applications.

Other jurisdictions like the US are developing their own approaches, with the recent Executive Order on AI introducing the concept of "dual-use foundation models" subject to additional oversight.

Global Governance Initiatives

The G7 Hiroshima AI Process has produced International Guiding Principles and a voluntary Code of Conduct for organizations developing advanced AI systems. Key principles include:

- Implementing risk assessment and mitigation measures throughout the AI lifecycle

- Enhancing transparency around AI capabilities and limitations

- Investing in security controls and safeguards

- Developing reliable content authentication mechanisms

- Prioritizing research on societal impacts and risk mitigation

These principles aim to establish a common baseline for responsible AI development globally.

Advancing a Risk-Based Approach

A risk-based regulatory framework for generative AI offers several advantages:

- **Proportionality:** Focuses strictest requirements on highest-risk applications

- **Flexibility:** Can adapt as technology evolves

- **Innovation-friendly:** Avoids overly prescriptive rules for lower-risk use cases

- **Clarity:** Provides legal certainty for different actors in the AI value chain

To be effective, risk-based frameworks should:

- Clearly define risk categories and assessment criteria

- Establish processes for ongoing monitoring and re-evaluation of risks

- Involve multistakeholder input in developing standards and best practices

- Promote international harmonization of approaches where possible

---

Recommendations

- Governments should adopt risk-based regulatory approaches for AI, focusing strictest oversight on high-risk applications while allowing flexibility for lower-risk use cases.

- Policymakers should develop clear, harmonized standards for AI risk assessment and mitigation, in collaboration with industry and civil society stakeholders.

- Ex-ante impact assessments should be required for AI systems deployed in sensitive domains or with potential for significant societal impact.

- International cooperation through forums like the G7 and OECD should be strengthened to promote alignment of AI governance frameworks globally.

- Governments should invest in AI safety research, workforce development, and public education to build capacity for effective AI governance.

Conclusion

As generative AI technologies continue to rapidly advance, establishing effective governance frameworks is crucial to realizing their benefits while mitigating risks. The risk-based approach emerging from initiatives like the EU AI Act and G7 Hiroshima Process offers a promising model for proportionate, innovation-friendly regulation. By promoting international coordination, multistakeholder collaboration, and ongoing adaptation of governance approaches, policymakers can work to ensure the responsible development and deployment of generative AI globally.

THIRTY NINE

AI Won't Be Safe Until We Rein in Big Tech

Georg Riekeles and Max von Thun, European Policy Studies,
November 2023

This report analyzes the pressing need to regulate Big Tech companies as a crucial step towards ensuring artificial intelligence (AI) safety and ethical development. Drawing primarily from the commentary "AI won't be safe until we rein in Big Tech" by Georg Riekeles and Max von Thun, we explore the challenges posed by the concentration of power in the hands of a few tech giants and its implications for AI safety.

The recent chaos at OpenAI, a leading AI research company, has highlighted the urgent need for stricter regulatory measures on large AI model providers. This incident underscores the need for more reliance on self-regulation and goodwill from companies whose accountability structures are often opaque and unreliable.

As AI plays an increasingly significant role in various aspects of society, ensuring its safe and ethical development becomes paramount. This report examines the current landscape of AI development and the role of Big

Tech in shaping this landscape and proposes regulatory approaches to address these challenges.

Key Findings

- The concentration of AI development among a few tech giants poses significant risks to safety and ethical considerations in AI.

- Self-regulation and voluntary agreements need to be revised to ensure responsible AI development and deployment.

- Effective AI safety measures require robust competition policy and strict regulatory obligations for dominant AI providers.

- While promising, the EU's efforts to regulate AI need further strengthening to address the challenges posed by large-scale AI models adequately.

- Imposing fiduciary duties on Big Tech companies could be a complementary approach to ensure they act in the public interest.

Analysis

The Concentration of AI Power

The commentary highlights how a handful of tech giants have leveraged their monopoly over computing power, data, and technical expertise to dominate the development of large-scale AI foundation models. This concentration of power raises several concerns:

- **Market Dominance:** Smaller companies often find themselves entering one-sided deals with or being acquired by larger players to gain access to necessary resources. Examples include Google's acquisition of DeepMind and Microsoft's partnership with OpenAI.

- **Lock-in Effects:** Tech giants can exploit their dominance in other markets, such as search engines, cloud computing, and browsers, to lock users into their AI models and services.

- **Network Effects:** As more users gravitate towards a few AI models and services, network effects and economies of scale further entrench the dominance of Big Tech.

- **Innovation Control:** The concentrated market for foundation models allows a handful of dominant corporations to steer the direction and speed of AI innovation.

The Inadequacy of Self-Regulation

Recent events, such as the turmoil at OpenAI, demonstrate the limitations of relying on self-regulation and voluntary agreements:

- **Lack of Accountability:** The governance structures of many AI companies, including those backed by

Big Tech, are often opaque and need clear accountability mechanisms.

- **Conflicting Interests:** There's an inherent tension between the profit motives of Big Tech companies and the need for responsible AI development.

- **Voluntary Measures:** The AI Safety Summit at Bletchley Park, while well-intentioned, resulted in vague commitments and voluntary agreements that lack real enforcement power.

Regulatory Approaches

The authors argue for a two-pronged approach to address these challenges:

Robust Competition Policy: Antitrust authorities should use their powers to prevent monopolistic practices in AI development. This includes:

- Investigating and breaking up anti-competitive deals between Big Tech and AI startups

- Preventing digital gatekeepers from leveraging their control over dominant platforms to entrench their hold on AI

Strict Regulatory Obligations: Given the limited number of foundation model providers, regulation must impose unprecedented responsibilities on dominant companies. Proposals include:

- Imposing fiduciary duties on AI providers, requiring them to act in the best interests of users and society

- Designating digital gatekeepers as public utilities, mandating fair treatment of customers and operational safety

The EU AI Act and Its Limitations

The report discusses the European Union's efforts to regulate AI through the EU AI Act. While this legislation is a step in the right direction, the authors argue that it needs strengthening:

- **Tiered Obligations:** The current proposal includes tiered obligations for foundation model providers, such as sharing information on training processes and submitting to audits for systemic risks.

- **Need for Stronger Measures:** The authors argue for stricter overarching responsibilities for dominant AI corporations to behave fairly and in the public interest.

Complementary Approach: Information Fiduciaries

As a supplementary concept, the idea of treating digital companies as "information fiduciaries" could complement the regulatory approaches suggested in the primary commentary:

- **Fiduciary Duties:** This model would impose duties of care, confidentiality, and loyalty on digital platforms that collect and use personal data.

- **Addressing Power Imbalances:** The fiduciary model could help address the vulnerabilities created by the power asymmetries between Big Tech companies and users.

- **Balancing Innovation and Protection:** This approach aims to allow continued innovation while imposing necessary guardrails against abusive practices.

Recommendations

- Policymakers should prioritize the enforcement of competition law in the AI sector to prevent further concentration of power among Big Tech companies.

- Regulators should impose strict obligations on dominant AI providers, including fiduciary duties and public utility-like responsibilities.

- The EU should strengthen its proposed AI Act to include more robust measures for regulating large-scale AI models and their providers.

- Policymakers should explore the implementation of the information fiduciary model as a complementary approach to regulating Big Tech's use of personal data in AI development.

- International cooperation should be pursued to develop global standards for AI safety and ethical development.

Conclusion

The safe and ethical development of AI is crucial as this technology becomes increasingly integrated into various aspects of society. However, the current concentration of AI power in the hands of a few Big Tech companies poses significant risks. Relying on self-regulation and voluntary measures has proven insufficient.

To ensure AI safety, it is imperative to rein in Big Tech through a combination of robust competition policy and strict regulatory obligations. By addressing the monopolistic tendencies in AI development and imposing clear responsibilities on dominant players, we can create an environment where AI can flourish while serving the public interest.

The EU's efforts to regulate AI provide a starting point, but they need to be strengthened and complemented by other approaches, such as the information fiduciary model. As we move forward, it is crucial to balance the need for innovation with the imperative of protecting societal interests and individual rights in the age of AI.

Further Reading

Riekeles, Georg and Max von Thun. "AI won't be safe until we rein in Big Tech." European Policy Centre, 2023.

Balkin, Jack M. "Information Fiduciaries and the First Amendment." UC Davis Law Review, 2016.

Zuboff, Shoshana. The Age of Surveillance Capitalism: The Fight for a Human Future at the New Frontier of Power. Profile Books, 2019.

European Commission. "Proposal for a Regulation laying down harmonised rules on artificial intelligence." April 2021.

Khan, Lina M. "Amazon's Antitrust Paradox." Yale Law Journal, 2017.

FORTY

The Drama at OpenAI Shows That AI Governance Remains in the Hands of a Select Few

Alex Krasodomski, Chatham House, November 2023

The recent upheaval at OpenAI, one of the world's leading artificial intelligence (AI) companies, has sent shockwaves through the tech industry and beyond. This report analyzes the events surrounding the unexpected firing and potential rehiring of CEO Sam Altman, and examines the broader implications for AI governance and development.

The chaos at OpenAI serves as a stark reminder that the control and direction of AI development remain concentrated in the hands of a select few tech leaders, companies, and investors. This concentration of power raises serious questions about the oversight and regulation of a technology that could fundamentally reshape our world.

As AI continues to advance at a breakneck pace, the events at OpenAI highlight the urgent need for more robust governance structures, increased public oversight, and a broader conversation about the future of AI development. This report explores the key issues raised by the OpenAI drama and offers recommendations for addressing the challenges of AI governance in an era of rapid technological change.

Key Findings

- The turmoil at OpenAI demonstrates that the gap between those driving AI development and the rest of society is widening, with critical decisions being made by a small group of individuals and companies.

- Microsoft emerged as a potential winner in the chaos, quickly moving to hire Altman and potentially strengthening its position in AI leadership.

- The events may represent a shift away from OpenAI's original mission-driven model toward faster, more profit-oriented development, raising concerns about the prioritization of safety and ethical considerations.

- Despite recent calls for caution and regulation, including at the UK's AI Safety Summit, the pace of AI development shows no signs of slowing.

- The OpenAI situation highlights the challenges of balancing rapid innovation with responsible development in the AI field.

- Public oversight and regulation of AI development are lagging far behind the pace of technological advancement, creating potential risks for society.

Analysis

Concentration of Power in AI Development

The OpenAI drama brings into sharp focus the extent to which decisions about AI development are concentrated among a small group of tech leaders, companies, and investors. As the article notes, "It is not humanity that gets to influence what might be the defining technology of the century. Rather it is a tiny cadre of technology leaders, billion-dollar companies and venture capitalists in control while regulation and public oversight lags behind."

This concentration of power raises serious concerns about accountability and representation in shaping the future of AI. With potential impacts spanning every aspect of human life, the direction of AI development should not be determined solely by a handful of individuals in Silicon Valley.

Governance Challenges and Competing Priorities

OpenAI's unique corporate structure, with a nonprofit board overseeing a for-profit arm, was designed to balance rapid development with safety considerations. However, the recent chaos suggests significant tensions within this model. The article points to a potential conflict between those focused on AI safety and alignment research, such as Chief Scientist Ilya Sutskever, and those pushing for faster commercial development and integration of AI technologies, possibly including Altman and investors.

This tension reflects a broader debate in the AI community about the appropriate pace of development and the prioritization of safety versus capability advancement. The events at OpenAI may indicate a shift towards prioritizing rapid development and commercialization over more cautious, safety-oriented approaches.

The Role of Big Tech in AI Governance

Microsoft's swift action to potentially hire Altman following his ousting from OpenAI highlights the significant influence of major tech companies in shaping the AI landscape. As the article notes, "The biggest winner looks to be Microsoft, whose CEO Satya Nadella's quick thinking has turned a potential disruption into a crushing victory."

This incident raises questions about the increasing consolidation of AI talent and resources within a few large tech companies. While this concentration may accelerate development, it also potentially reduces diversity of approaches and concentrates decision-making power even further.

Lack of Regulation and Public Oversight

A crucial issue highlighted by the OpenAI situation is the significant lag between AI development and regulatory frameworks. As the article states, "regulation and public oversight lags behind" the rapid pace of AI advancement. This gap creates potential risks as powerful AI systems are developed and deployed without adequate safeguards or public input.

The need for effective regulation is becoming increasingly urgent as AI systems take on more significant roles in society. However, the complexity and rapid evolution of AI technology present significant challenges for regulators attempting to keep pace.

Risks of Rapid AI Development

While the article does not delve deeply into existential risks often associated with advanced AI, it does highlight real near-term risks of AI systems making consequential decisions without adequate safeguards. Examples cited include AI-enabled tools automatically rejecting certain demographics in recruitment and accidents involving self-driving cars.

These examples underscore the potential for AI systems to have significant real-world impacts, even in their current state of development. As AI capabilities continue to advance, the potential consequences of errors or misuse become even more severe.

The Struggle Between Idealism and Market Forces

The article suggests that the OpenAI drama could be seen as "a fight between an idealistic governance model (designed to put mission before profit) and the realities of the tech sector—a fight in which the idealistic model appears to have lost." This framing highlights the challenges of maintaining a focus on safety and ethical considerations in an environment driven by market forces and the pursuit of technological dominance.

The apparent victory of commercial interests over the original mission-driven model at OpenAI raises concerns about the future direction of AI development across the industry. It suggests that economic incentives may be overriding careful consideration of long-term consequences and ethical implications.

Global Implications of AI Development

While the article focuses primarily on events in Silicon Valley, the implications of these developments are global. AI technology developed by a handful of companies in the United States has the potential to impact individuals and societies worldwide. This raises important questions about global governance of AI and the need for international cooperation in shaping the future of this technology.

Recommendations

- Develop more robust and inclusive governance structures for AI development that incorporate a wider range of stakeholders, including ethicists, social scientists, and representatives from diverse communities.

- Accelerate the development of regulatory frameworks for AI, with a focus on ensuring safety, protecting individual rights, and promoting ethical development practices.

- Encourage greater transparency in AI development processes, including regular public reporting on safety measures and ethical considerations.

- Invest in AI safety and alignment research at levels commensurate with investments in capability advancements.

- Implement stronger testing and validation processes for AI systems before widespread deployment, especially for applications with significant societal impacts.

- Foster international cooperation on AI governance, recognizing the global implications of AI development.

- Promote diversity in AI development teams and leadership to ensure a wider range of perspectives are considered in decision-making processes.

- Develop educational programs to increase public understanding of AI technology and its implications, enabling more informed public participation in debates about AI governance.

- Explore alternative corporate structures and incentive models that better align the interests of AI companies with broader societal benefits.

- Establish independent oversight bodies with the expertise and authority to monitor and evaluate high-stakes AI development projects.

Conclusion

The drama at OpenAI serves as a wake-up call, highlighting the urgent need for more robust governance structures in

AI development. As AI technology continues to advance at a rapid pace, it is crucial that we address the concentration of power in the hands of a select few and work towards more inclusive, transparent, and accountable models of AI development.

The potential benefits of AI are enormous, but so too are the risks if development proceeds without adequate oversight and consideration of long-term consequences. By implementing stronger governance frameworks, investing in safety research, and broadening participation in key decisions, we can work towards ensuring that AI development proceeds in a manner that benefits humanity as a whole.

The events at OpenAI demonstrate that we are at a critical juncture in the development of AI technology. The choices made now by companies, regulators, and society at large will shape the trajectory of AI for years to come. It is imperative that we rise to this challenge and establish governance structures that can guide AI development towards outcomes that are safe, ethical, and beneficial for all.

Further Reading

Bostrom, Nick. "Superintelligence: Paths, Dangers, Strategies." Oxford University Press, 2014.

Russell, Stuart. "Human Compatible: Artificial Intelligence and the Problem of Control." Viking, 2019.

European Commission. "Proposal for a Regulation on Artificial Intelligence." April 2021.

Crawford, Kate. "Atlas of AI: Power, Politics, and the Planetary Costs of Artificial Intelligence." Yale University Press, 2021.

Tegmark, Max. "Life 3.0: Being Human in the Age of Artificial Intelligence." Knopf, 2017.

FORTY ONE

The Global Race for Artificial Intelligence Regulation

Enzo Maria Le Fevre Cervini, Istituto per gli Studi di Politica Internazionale, November 2023

This report analyzes the recent flurry of international activity around artificial intelligence (AI) regulation, highlighting how AI governance has become a global priority. In the span of just a few weeks, major international bodies and world powers have issued statements or taken legislative actions emphasizing the importance of ethics and regulation in the rapidly advancing field of AI. This report examines these developments, their implications, and the emerging global landscape of AI governance.

The rapid pace of AI development and its potential to transform numerous sectors of society have created an urgent need for regulatory frameworks to ensure the technology is developed and deployed responsibly. However, the global nature of AI development presents challenges for creating cohesive international governance structures. This report explores how different actors are approaching these challenges and the potential for international cooperation on AI regulation.

Key Findings

- Multiple major international bodies and world powers have recently issued statements or taken actions on AI regulation, including the UN, G7, US, UK, and EU.

- There is broad agreement on the need for ethical and responsible AI development, with emphasis on human rights, security, and data protection.

- International cooperation is seen as crucial for addressing the global challenges posed by AI.

- Differences exist in regulatory approaches, with some actors favoring more stringent rules while others emphasize flexibility.

- The regulation of advanced "frontier AI" systems is emerging as a particular area of focus.

- Efforts are being made to include diverse stakeholders in AI governance discussions.

Analysis

United Nations High-level Advisory Body on Artificial Intelligence

In recent months, the UN Secretary-General initiated the creation of a High-level Advisory Body on Artificial Intelligence. This multi-stakeholder body brings together 39 experts from governments, the private sector, and civil society worldwide. Its mandate is to analyze the current state of AI development and make recommendations for international AI governance.

Key aspects of this initiative include:

- **Diverse perspectives:** The advisory body includes a wide range of stakeholders, ensuring multiple viewpoints are considered.

- **Focus on common good:** The group is tasked with exploring how AI can be governed for the benefit of humanity as a whole.

- **Alignment with UN goals:** Recommendations are expected to take into account human rights and the Sustainable Development Goals.

This UN initiative represents an important step towards creating a truly global framework for AI governance. By bringing together diverse experts from around the world, it has the potential to develop recommendations that are both comprehensive and widely applicable.

G7 Leaders' Statement on the Hiroshima AI Process

On October 30, 2023, the G7 issued a statement on AI as part of the Hiroshima AI Process. This statement emphasizes several key points:

- **Ethical development:** The G7 countries assert that AI should be developed, adopted, and used in a manner that respects principles of ethics, trust, and responsibility.

- **Human rights and security:** The statement acknowledges the importance of considering human rights, security, and data protection in AI development and deployment.

- **International cooperation:** The G7 emphasizes the need for collaboration among nations to address AI challenges.

- **Comprehensive approach:** The statement underscores the importance of addressing ethical considerations across all aspects of AI development and use.

The G7 statement is significant as it represents a consensus among some of the world's most powerful economies on the need for ethical AI development. However, it remains to be seen how these principles will be translated into concrete policies and actions.

US Executive Order on Safe, Secure, and Trustworthy Artificial Intelligence

On the same day as the G7 statement, President Biden issued an executive order on AI. This order establishes new standards for AI safety and protection in the United States, with several key provisions:

- **Safety and protection standards:** The order sets new benchmarks for AI safety and user protection.

- **Privacy safeguards:** These include measures to protect the privacy of American citizens.

- **Equity and civil rights:** The order promotes equity and defends civil rights in AI applications.

- **Consumer and worker protection:** Includes provisions to safeguard consumers and workers from potential AI-related harms.

- **Innovation and competition:** The order aims to foster innovation and competition in the AI sector.

- **Global leadership:** It seeks to advance American leadership in AI on the global stage.

This executive order represents a significant step in AI regulation for the United States, setting a comprehensive framework for responsible AI development and use. Given the US's prominent role in AI development, its focus on domestic policy could influence global standards.

The Bletchley Declaration on AI Safety

Two days after the US executive order, 28 governments and the European Union signed The Bletchley Declaration on AI safety at the UK-hosted AI Security Summit. Key aspects of this declaration include:

- **Focus on "frontier AI":** The declaration specifically addresses highly capable AI systems that could pose significant risks.

- **Risk recognition:** It acknowledges both the opportunities and potential dangers associated with advanced AI.

- **International cooperation:** The declaration emphasizes the need for global collaboration to address AI risks.

- **Specific risk areas:** It highlights concerns related to areas such as cybersecurity and biotechnology.

- **Timely action:** The declaration stresses the importance of understanding AI risks and promptly addressing them.

The Bletchley Declaration is notable for its focus on advanced AI systems and its broad international support. It represents an important step towards global cooperation on AI safety, particularly for cutting-edge technologies.

Comparative Analysis

While these various initiatives and declarations share many common themes, there are also important differences in their approaches:

- **Scope and focus:** The UN initiative takes the broadest view, seeking to develop global governance recommendations. The G7 statement focuses on principles for G7 nations, while the US executive order is primarily concerned with domestic policy. The Bletchley Declaration sits somewhere in between, with a multinational focus but emphasis on specific advanced AI systems.

- **Regulatory approach:** The US executive order suggests more stringent rules and standards, while the G7 statement and Bletchley Declaration allow for more flexibility in implementation.

- **Stakeholder involvement:** All initiatives emphasize the importance of involving diverse stakeholders, but the UN advisory body is the most explicitly multi-stakeholder in its composition.

- **Timeframe and concreteness:** The US executive order provides the most immediate and concrete actions, while the other initiatives focus on setting principles and directions for future policy development.

Other Regional Initiatives

In addition to these major international efforts, there have been important regional initiatives:

- **Latin America and the Caribbean:** The "Declaración de Santiago" issued at a UNESCO-promoted summit addresses AI challenges specific to the region, with a focus on issues like gender equality and inclusion.

- **Spain:** As part of its EU Council Presidency, Spain has moved to establish a National Agency for AI Supervision, potentially setting a model for other European countries.

These regional efforts highlight the importance of tailoring AI governance approaches to specific local contexts and needs.

Recommendations

- **Foster international cooperation:** Given the global nature of AI development and its potential impacts, continued efforts to build international consensus and cooperation on AI governance are crucial.

- **Balance innovation and regulation:** Regulatory frameworks should aim to promote responsible AI development without stifling innovation. Flexible, principle-based approaches may be more effective than rigid rules.

- **Focus on high-risk areas:** Special attention should be given to regulating advanced "frontier AI" systems that pose the greatest potential risks.

- **Promote stakeholder inclusion:** Efforts should be made to include diverse voices, including those from developing countries and underrepresented groups, in AI governance discussions.

- **Develop concrete implementation plans:** While high-level principles are important, there is a need to translate these into specific, actionable policies and regulations.

- **Address regional specificities:** While working towards global standards, allowing for regional variations that address specific local needs and contexts is important.

- **Invest in AI literacy:** Governments and international organizations should promote public understanding of AI to enable informed participation in governance discussions.

Conclusion

The recent flurry of activity around AI regulation demonstrates that this has become a global priority. There is broad agreement on the need for ethical, responsible AI development that respects human rights and promotes the common good. However, significant challenges still need to be solved in translating these principles into effective governance structures.

The diversity of approaches being taken–from the UN's global advisory body to national initiatives like the US executive order–reflects the complexity of the issue. While this diversity can lead to valuable experimentation and tailored solutions, it also risks creating a fragmented regulatory landscape.

Moving forward, the key challenge will be to balance the need for global coordination with the flexibility to address local and regional specificities. Continued international dialogue and cooperation will be crucial to developing effective, widely accepted frameworks for AI governance.

As AI technology continues to advance rapidly, the race to develop appropriate regulatory frameworks takes on increasing urgency. The actions taken in the coming months and years will play a crucial role in shaping the future of AI and its impacts on society. It is imperative that these efforts continue to prioritize ethical considerations, human rights, and the common good as we navigate the complex landscape of AI governance.

Further Reading

United Nations. "Secretary-General's High-level Advisory Body on Artificial Intelligence." 2023.

G"G7 Leaders' Statement on the Hiroshima AI Process." October 30, 2023.

The White House. "Executive Order on Safe, Secure, and Trustworthy Artificial Intelligence." October 30, 2023.

UK Government. "The Bletchley Declaration by Countries Attending the AI Safety Summit." November 1, 2023.

UNESCO. "Declaración de Santiago sobre Inteligencia Artificial y Desarrollo Sostenible en América Latina y el Caribe." October 24, 2023.

FORTY TWO

Awareness of Artificial Intelligence: Diffusion of information about AI versus ChatGPT in the United States

Rajeev K. Goel and Michael A. Nelson, Kiel Institute for the World Economy, November 2023

This report analyzes the drivers of awareness about artificial intelligence (AI) across US states, distinguishing between general AI awareness and awareness specifically about ChatGPT. The research creates unique indices of Google search results for each state to quantify AI awareness, providing insights into how information about this rapidly evolving technology is spreading. Understanding the factors influencing AI awareness is crucial for policymakers as they consider regulatory approaches and ways to promote responsible AI development.

Key Findings

- More prosperous states had greater awareness about both general AI and ChatGPT, likely due to greater affordability and access to internet technologies.

- States with greater economic freedom showed lower AI awareness, possibly because fewer regulations create less demand for AI services as alternative business options.

- The influence of gender ratios varied based on how awareness was measured, suggesting complex relationships between gender and AI engagement.

- States with higher urbanization showed greater AI awareness when measured relative to land area, but not when measured per internet user.

- The proportion of elderly population did not significantly impact AI awareness.

- States bordering Mexico generally had lower AI awareness, while those bordering Canada showed no significant difference.

Analysis

Measuring AI Awareness

The study created two unique indices to measure AI awareness in each state:

- **General AI awareness:** Google search results for "How to use AI OR artificial intelligence" + state name

- **ChatGPT-specific awareness:** Google search results for "How to use ChatGPT OR AI" + state name

These search results were normalized in two ways:

a) Per square mile of state land area

b) Per estimated number of internet users in the state

This approach allows for analysis of both general and specific AI awareness while accounting for differences in state size and internet penetration.

Key Drivers of AI Awareness

Economic Factors:

- Per capita income showed a strong positive relationship with AI awareness, especially when normalized by land area. A 1% increase in per capita income correlated with a 4% increase in general AI awareness and a 5% increase in ChatGPT awareness.

- Economic freedom, measured by an index of state-level regulations, had a negative relationship with AI awareness. States with less regulation showed lower levels of AI-related internet searches.

Demographic and Geographic Factors:

- Gender ratios produced mixed results. States with more men relative to women showed lower AI awareness when measured per land area, but higher awareness when measured per internet user.

- Urbanization positively correlated with AI awareness when measured per land area, but showed no significant relationship when measured per internet user.

- The proportion of elderly population did not significantly impact AI awareness.

- States bordering Mexico showed lower AI awareness, while those bordering Canada were not significantly different from other states.

Variations Across the AI Awareness Spectrum:

Quantile regression analysis revealed that the influence of various factors on AI awareness varied depending on the overall level of awareness in a state:

- The impact of determinants was generally stronger, both in magnitude and statistical significance, in states with higher levels of AI awareness.

- This suggests there may be a threshold level of awareness, above which policy interventions could have greater impact.

- Results were generally stronger when awareness was measured relative to land area rather than per internet user.

Recommendations

- Target awareness-building efforts in less prosperous states to bridge the AI knowledge gap.

- Consider the potential unintended consequences of economic deregulation on AI awareness and adoption.

- Develop tailored strategies to promote AI awareness that account for demographic differences, particularly related to gender and urbanization.

- Focus initial policy efforts on states with higher baseline levels of AI awareness, where interventions may have greater impact.

- Investigate and address the factors contributing to lower AI awareness in states bordering Mexico.

- Develop more nuanced measures of AI awareness that can capture qualitative differences in understanding and engagement with AI technologies.

- Conduct longitudinal studies to track how AI awareness evolves over time and in response to major technological developments or policy changes.

- Explore the relationship between AI awareness and actual AI adoption or implementation across different sectors of the economy.

254 • AI DIGEST VOL 2

Conclusion

The diffusion of AI awareness across US states shows significant variation driven by economic, demographic, and geographic factors. As AI technologies continue to advance rapidly, understanding these patterns of awareness is crucial for developing effective policies to promote responsible AI development and adoption. The findings suggest that a one-size-fits-all approach to AI policy may need to be revised, and that targeted strategies accounting for state-level differences may be necessary to ensure equitable access to and understanding of AI technologies.

Further Research

Agrawal, A., Gans, J., & Goldfarb, A. (2018). Prediction Machines: The Simple Economics of Artificial Intelligence. Harvard Business Review Press.

Brynjolfsson, E., & McAfee, A. (2017). The Business of Artificial Intelligence. Harvard Business Review, July-August 2017.

West, D. M. (2018). The Future of Work: Robots, AI, and Automation. Brookings Institution Press.

Acemoglu, D., & Restrepo, P. (2019). Automation and New Tasks: How Technology Displaces and Reinstates Labor. Journal of Economic Perspectives, 33(2), 3-30.

Goel, R. K., & Nelson, M. A. (2021). How do firms use artificial intelligence? A study across industries. Managerial and Decision Economics, 42(4), 1020-1034.

FORTY THREE

The Geopolitics of Generative AI: international implications and the role of the European Union

Raquel Jorge Ricart and Pau Álvarez-Aragonés, Real Institute Elcano, November 2024

This report analyzes the geopolitical implications of generative artificial intelligence (AI), focusing on the international competition to develop and deploy this transformative technology. Generative AI enables machines to create new content, such as text, images, and code, has emerged as a key battleground in the global technology race. While offering immense economic potential, generative AI also raises significant security, privacy, and ethics concerns that demand careful governance approaches.

This analysis examines generative AI development across major powers, assesses its anticipated impacts across key domains, and evaluates policy responses focusing on the European Union's role. By synthesizing insights from multiple recent studies and policy documents, it aims to provide a comprehensive overview of this rapidly evolving technological and geopolitical landscape.

Key Findings

- The United States and China are leading in generative AI development, and they compete intensely but also collaborate on an ongoing basis.

- US companies dominate in terms of market capitalization and venture capital investment, while China leads in patent applications.

- Generative AI is expected to have major economic impacts, potentially adding trillions to global GDP, but also disrupting labor markets.

- Security implications include both opportunities for defense/intelligence applications and risks around misinformation and cyberattacks.

- Many countries and international bodies are developing AI governance frameworks, with the EU taking a proactive regulatory approach.

- The EU needs to catch up in generative AI development and investment, but aims to shape global standards through regulation and diplomacy.

Analysis

State of Generative AI Development and Competition

The global race to develop generative AI capabilities has primarily become a competition between the United States and China, though with continued collaboration between researchers and companies in both countries. According to data compiled by the Elcano Royal Institute, the number of US-China AI research collaborations increased roughly four times from 2010 to 2021, though the pace of growth has slowed recently.

In terms of private sector development, US companies currently hold a strong lead. The top generative AI firms by market capitalization are dominated by American tech giants, with Microsoft ($2.44 trillion) and Alphabet ($1.72 trillion) in the lead. The highest-ranked Chinese company, Alibaba, comes in 7th at $242 billion. US firms also have key advantages in critical hardware like graphics processing units (GPUs) and cloud computing infrastructure essential for training large AI models.

However, China holds a decisive lead in AI-related patent applications. In 2022, China filed 29,853 AI-related patents, accounting for over 40% of the global total. This compares to 1,416 patent applications from the US, making up 19.8% of the total. Since 2017, China's cumulative AI patent applications have surpassed those of the US.

Venture capital investment tells a different story, with the US attracting the lion's share of funding. Since 2019, generative AI startups have raised over $28.3 billion globally. In 2023 alone, they attracted $17.8 billion from January to August. Notably, 89% of global generative AI venture funding has gone to US-based startups.

The intensity of this technological race is spurring increased government involvement. In the US, President Biden recently issued an Executive Order on "Safe, Secure, and Trustworthy Artificial Intelligence" which aims to promote AI innovation while establishing guardrails around safety and ethics. China has also moved to regulate the sector, with the Cyberspace Administration of China releasing draft rules on generative AI in July 2023.

Economic and Labor Market Impacts

The potential economic impact of generative AI is immense, though estimates vary. According to Goldman Sachs, generative AI could drive a 7% (or almost $7 trillion) increase in global GDP and lift productivity growth by 1.5 percentage points over a 10-year period. Similarly, McKinsey estimates that generative AI could add between $2.6 trillion to $4.4 trillion in value annually across various industries.

This economic transformation would be accompanied by significant labor market disruption. Generative AI is expected to impact knowledge work and decision-making roles that were previously less susceptible to automation. McKinsey's survey found that 38% of organizations expect to reskill over 20% of their workforce due to AI adoption. In some areas like service operations, the majority of respondents anticipated workforce decreases.

However, the ultimate impact on inequality remains uncertain. Some experts argue that because generative AI operates on language and can mimic higher-level skills, it may be the first form of automation that could potentially reduce rather than increase inequality. This will depend greatly on how the technology is implemented and governed.

Security and Defense Implications

Generative AI presents both opportunities and risks in the security and defense domains. Military and intelligence agencies are exploring its potential for enhancing situational awareness, decision-making, and scenario planning. However, the reliance of many generative AI systems on open-source data and platforms raises concerns about their reliability for sensitive applications.

The dual-use nature of generative AI technologies is apparent in areas like drone development. Chinese companies like DJI dominate the commercial drone market, holding a 70% global market share. As generative AI capabilities are integrated into drone systems, this could have significant implications for both civilian and military applications.

Major security risks associated with generative AI include:

- Creation of highly convincing deepfakes for disinformation campaigns

- Generation of malicious code to enable more sophisticated cyberattacks

- Privacy and data security concerns as AI systems process vast amounts of personal information

NATO and other defense organizations are actively studying these issues. NATO's Data and Artificial Intelligence Review Board has hosted briefings on generative AI's potential impact, concluding that current systems are not yet sufficiently advanced for critical military functions but warrant close monitoring.

Global Governance Approaches

As generative AI capabilities rapidly advance, governments and international bodies are racing to develop appropriate governance frameworks. Some key initiatives include:

- The UN Secretary-General established a High-Level Advisory Body on Artificial Intelligence, bringing together 39 experts to make recommendations on global AI governance.

- The G7's Hiroshima AI Process produced a statement on International Guiding Principles and a voluntary Code of Conduct for AI development.

- The OECD's AI Principles guide trustworthy AI that respects human rights and democratic values.

- China's draft rules on generative AI services focused on content monitoring and alignment with "core socialist values."

The EU's Role and Policy Approach

The European Union, while lagging behind the US and China in generative AI development, is taking a proactive approach to regulation and global standard-setting. Key elements of the EU's strategy include:

- **The AI Act:** This proposed regulation takes a risk-based approach to AI governance, with stricter rules for high-risk applications. The European Parliament has pushed for specific provisions on generative AI, including transparency requirements.

- **Economic Security Strategy:** The EU has identified AI as a critical technology area in its new economic security framework. It aims to reduce strategic dependencies and promote "de-risking" rather than decoupling from global supply chains.

- **International Partnerships:** The EU is leveraging its regulatory influence (the "Brussels effect") and pursuing tech diplomacy to shape global AI governance. This includes bilateral partnerships like the EU-US Trade and Technology Council and engagement in multilateral forums.

- **Research and Investment:** While the EU is behind in private-sector AI development, it promotes research and innovation through programs like Horizon Europe and national recovery plans. However, many experts argue that more aggressive investment is needed to close the gap with the US and China.

The EU faces several challenges in implementing its AI strategy:

- Balancing innovation and regulation: There are concerns that overly restrictive rules could hamper EU competitiveness in AI development.

- Fragmentation: Ensuring consistent implementation of AI rules across member states will be crucial.

- Global influence: While the EU aims to set global standards, its limited market power in AI may reduce its leverage.

Recommendations

- Increase public and private investment in generative AI research and development to narrow the gap with global leaders.

- Foster stronger linkages between European research institutions and industry to accelerate the commercialization of AI innovations.

- Leverage the EU's diplomatic weight to promote international cooperation on AI governance, particularly around high-risk applications and ethical standards.

- Ensure that the final AI Act strikes an appropriate balance between safeguarding rights and fostering innovation, with flexible mechanisms to adapt to rapid technological change.

- Develop comprehensive strategies to address the labor market impacts of generative AI, including reskilling programs and exploration of new economic models.

- Strengthen Europe's digital infrastructure, particularly in areas like cloud computing and semiconductor production, to support advanced AI development.

- Promote public awareness and understanding of generative AI to build trust and facilitate responsible adoption across society.

Conclusion

Generative AI represents a transformative technology with far-reaching geopolitical implications. While the United States and China currently lead in development, the ultimate impact of this technology will depend on how it is governed and deployed globally. The European Union, despite lagging in some areas, has an opportunity to play a crucial role in shaping ethical and human-centric approaches to AI.

As generative AI capabilities continue to advance at a rapid pace, policymakers must work to harness its immense potential while mitigating risks to security, privacy, and social cohesion. International cooperation will be essential to develop common standards and best practices. The decisions made in the coming years regarding AI governance will play a major role in shaping the global technological and economic landscape for decades to come.

Further Reading

Agrawal, Ajay, Joshua Gans, and Avi Goldfarb. "The Economics of Artificial Intelligence: An Agenda." University of Chicago Press, 2019.

European Commission. "Proposal for a Regulation laying down harmonised rules on artificial intelligence." April 2021.

Horowitz, Michael C., Gregory C. Allen, Elsa B. Kania, and Paul Scharre. "Strategic Competition in an Era of Artificial Intelligence." Center for a New American Security, 2018.

Lee, Kai-Fu. "AI Superpowers: China, Silicon Valley, and the New World Order." Houghton Mifflin Harcourt, 2018.

OECD. "Artificial Intelligence in Society." OECD Publishing, 2019.

Index

www.ingramcontent.com/pod-product-compliance
Lightning Source LLC
Chambersburg PA
CBHW071238050326
40690CB00011B/2163